Praise for *Peregrine Spring*

Peregrine Spring is "a roller coaster ride of experiences . . . an exquisite, moving, important and surprising book. . . . When the tempo does slow, it is a respite that gives the reader a chance to savor descriptions of incredibly beautiful birds which carry the reader along on their spectacular flights."
—Sy Montgomery, author of *The Soul of the Octopus*

"*Peregrine Spring* must be told. It is important that this book be published. People need to read this."
—Elizabeth Marshall Thomas, author of *The Hidden Life of Dogs*

"Nancy Cowan's *Peregrine Spring* is the best narrative of a modern falconer's life I know. It's not a how-to, though you can learn plenty from it. Nor does Nancy pose as an all-knowing 'Master,' though she is a master—or mistress—of our ancient practice. What she does give us is a falconry pilgrim's progress, from beginner to teacher, with all the thrills and delights and sometimes horrors that accompany the journey. I plan to give this book to every person who approaches me and wishes to become a falconer. It's essential."
—Steve Bodio, author of *A Rage for Falcons* and *Eagle Dreams*

"*Peregrine Spring* is a wonderful and often poignant account of Nancy Cowan's relationship with a host of raptors; their lives, personalities, and species-related abilities. This book is for those interested in human-animal relationships and future falconers alike."
—Ben Kilham, author of *Out on a Limb: What Black Bears Have Taught Me about Intelligence and Intuition*

"Cowan gives us striking insights into the inner workings of the relationships between raptors and their handlers, as only someone who has dedicated her life to these birds could do."
—Irene Pepperberg, author of *Alex & Me: How a Scientist and a Parrot Discovered a Hidden World of Animal Intelligence—and Formed a Deep Bond in the Process*

"Of all the working partnerships between humans and animals, the most intriguing and unfathomable must be the one between falconers and their birds. In this beguiling memoir, Nancy Cowan describes the knife's edge on which she and her fellow falconers balance—studying everything from medieval techniques to modern medicine, doing their best to understand the kinds of birds who think, but not the way we do; who accept their jesses and hoods, but don't lose their essential wildness; and who, when released into the sky, can at any time disappear and never return. Filled with information, beautiful descriptions, and stories both heartwarming and hair-raising, this is a book that will fascinate readers of all kinds."

—Suzie Gilbert, author of *Flyaway: How a Wild Bird Rehabber Sought Adventure and Found Her Wings*

"Since time immemorial, humans have looked to the skies and marveled at the flying skills and hunting prowess of falcons and hawks. We have craved the freedom of flight and the vicarious thrill of the kill. For thousands of years, falconry has allowed that thrill to manifest in the close union of bird and human. It's an uneasy alliance that requires patience, skill and care, and Nancy Cowan is one in a small number of practicing falconers today who share their passion and avocation with a wide audience. . . . Through *Peregrine Spring* we can all sail on the wind with Nancy's birds and take a glimpse into her life: a life devoted to an ancient art with a modern twist."

—Iain MacLeod, executive director, Squam Lakes Natural Science Center

"Not only does Nancy share the technical aspects of training and hunting a raptor, she brings to life the critical bond between falconer and falcon. A great read for anyone who wants to get a close look at what lies behind the curtain of falconry."

—Michael J. Bartlett, president, New Hampshire Audubon

"'How could anyone relate to a creature as cold and emotionless as a bird of prey?' asks Nancy Cowan in this marvelous book. She answers in stories steeped in admiration, learning and love. 'I have to do this right,' she tells herself about falconry. And she does. She gets her wordsmithing right, too, showing us the hearts of hunters in clean, feather-elegant prose that borders on poetry. Thank you, Nancy. My library is enriched by *Peregrine Spring*."

—Kim Heacox, author of *The Only Kayak* and *Rhythm of the Wild*

"Falconers will find many similarities to their own experiences in the recounting of Nancy's life. . . . Falconers, especially East Coast ones, will be able to identify many of our fellow falconers whom Nancy only identifies by their first names. It makes you feel like an insider and adds to the enjoyment of Nancy's story."

—Peter Barry Devers, director of the Falconry Heritage Trust

PEREGRINE SPRING

A Master Falconer's Extraordinary Life with Birds of Prey

NANCY COWAN

FOREWORD BY SY MONTGOMERY AND

ELIZABETH MARSHALL THOMAS

Guilford, Connecticut

An imprint of Rowman & Littlefield

Distributed by NATIONAL BOOK NETWORK

British Library Cataloguing in Publication Information Available

Library of Congress Cataloging-in-Publication Data

Names: Cowan, Nancy, author.
Title: Peregrine spring : a master falconer's extraordinary life with birds of prey / Nancy Cowan ;
    foreword by Sy Montgomery and Elizabeth Marshall Thomas.
Description: Guilford, Connecticut : Lyons Press, 2016.
Identifiers: LCCN 2015034745
Subjects: LCSH: Cowan, Nancy. | Falconers—United States—Biography. | Falconry. | Birds of
    prey.
Classification: LCC SK17.C64 A3 2016 | DDC 639.97/896092—dc23 LC record available at
    http://lccn.loc.gov/2015034745

ISBN 978-1-4930-1770-6 (cloth: alk. paper)
ISBN 978-1-4930-2997-6 (pbk : alk. paper)
ISBN 978-1-4930-1837-6 (electronic)

♾™ The paper used in this publication meets the minimum requirements of American National Standard for Information Sciences—Permanence of Paper for Printed Library Materials, ANSI/ NISO Z39.48-1992.

For Robert S. Gault, Elsie Dietrich Gault, and Margaret Gault Young,
who together came to me in a dream and promised Peregrine Spring *would*
be published. And for Jim, who is my past, my now, and my always.

CONTENTS

Part Three: A Life Filled with Raptors

Acknowledgments

Modern falconers have thousands of years of predecessors to thank for the expertise guiding us today. I have Jim Cowan, who shared his knowledge and love of raptors. Sy Montgomery, Elizabeth Marshall Thomas, and Selinda Chiquoine encouraged me tirelessly. My agent, Jacqueline Flynn, took me under her wing as a sponsor mentors an apprentice. My editor, Holly Rubino, provided, over and over, the one word I had been seeking when I scribed out dozens of sentences to say the same thing. To those with the forethought to take photos through the years, and to magnanimously allow their use, I owe my great appreciation. To countless falconers and to these persons who helped make *Peregrine Spring* a reality, I am deeply and lovingly grateful.

Foreword

by Sy Montgomery and
Elizabeth Marshall Thomas

Nancy Cowan and her hawks opened the sky to us.

We had both known birds before. We'd lived with cockatiels, chickens, lovebirds, parrots. And we had both studied and been stalked by predators. In the course of our work, one of us was followed by a leopard; the other was hunted by a swimming tiger. But before meeting Nancy, neither one of us knew what it was like to hold a lightning storm, a waterfall, a flaming comet on our glove—and then watch that fiery force fly from us to pierce other birds like an arrow.

Falconry, Nancy told us, is not just a sport, but an art, a science, and a passion—one that very few people understand. "Some people think, 'Nancy owns this bird, so it's a pet,'" Nancy said. "Or they have a mystical outlook: 'This bird loves me.'"

"Some people see the bird as an ornament," Nancy continued. "They are thinking how cool they will look with one on their arm. But," she explained, "the only people who really understand birds of prey are people who have worked with them for a long time. And every time I work with them, I learn something new. You accept that your life will be changed by being a falconer."

Nancy's relationship with her birds is utterly different from that of a person and her pet. It's a partnership unlike any either of us have experienced with any other animal, tame or wild. And yes, it changed our lives.

It will change yours, too. You, lucky reader, are about to learn the extraordinary story of a master falconer who not only changed our lives, but made New Hampshire history. Nancy and her amazing husband, Jim, made falconry legal in our state and established the New Hampshire School of Falconry. On a cool, gray, mid-October day, Sy became her first student.

That first lesson was a revelation. From the shocking strength of the grip of the huge yellow feet of the Harris's hawk on the glove, to the sharpness of the ebony talons, to the devouring look in the huge, mahogany eyes, nothing you can hold so close can embody the spirit of wildness, the pure fire of instinct, as a hawk. Nancy told us that day these birds don't think the way we think; they don't learn the way we do.

"To be in the gripping gaze of that bird was like looking directly into the sun," Sy wrote to our mutual friend, the poet Howard Nelson. Nancy showed us how hawks live through their eyes even more than we do. And when hooded, it's like their souls are turned off. You take off the hood and the soul returns to the bird. They are all pure instinct. They live utterly, purely, densely in the moment, here, now, and nowhere else—because really there *is* nowhere else.

That first lesson, October 18, 2005, led to dozens of others. Sy's beloved chickens prevented her from keeping a hawk herself—but did not dim her love of these incandescent beings, or from spreading the word about Nancy's School of Falconry. She wrote about Nancy in her book, *Birdology*, and also brought Liz to take lessons as well.

Liz came for the first time in January 2006. She loved it. You start by wearing a long, heavy glove on your left hand, in which you grasp some kind of bait such as a dead baby chick. You must then turn your back to the hawk, extending your gloved arm. When the hawk lands, you bring your arm around so you and she can face each other, but before that you should watch her approach in case she does something unexpected. So you must turn your face away and watch from the corners of your eyes because your eyes should be as far from her oncoming claws as possible.

Nancy explained why. "That is how many hawks kill their prey," she said in a casual manner, "forcing their talons through the skull via the eye socket into the brain. If they think there is any chance the food might go away, they fly into your face and go for your eyes."

A statement like that gets one's attention. Perhaps a little scared, Liz followed Nancy's instructions. She turned her back so her face wouldn't get involved, took care to look over her shoulder, used her peripheral vision to spot the hawk who was in a tree, and only then held out her gloved arm. The hawk spread her wings and flew toward her.

The Harris's hawk's name was Fire. She was the issue of a dinosaur like *Tyrannosaurus rex* who walked on its hind legs but was smaller. When this marvelous female landed on Liz's arm, her dinosaur claws gripped the glove. She found the bait and gulped it. She then turned to see whose glove she was gripping and saw a flat, naked face with no fur or feathers and a pair of plain-looking eyes much like those of any other animal. The face was in motion—the lips slightly parting, the nostrils slightly quivering, the eyebrows slightly raising, and the plain-looking eyes opening wide. The owner of the face seemed entranced.

Liz, in contrast, saw a hooked beak, two static nostrils, and magnificent shining eyes that could see for miles and seemed to have the world inside them. But like the dinosaur that made this hawk, a bird has no muscles in its face, and Fire's expression showed nothing.

Of course Liz wanted more. *Please, Gaia*, she begged, *I'm just a mammal. Everything I know comes from watching other faces. But here's this hawk whose face doesn't move. How can I understand her?*

And Gaia said, *I made that face a long time ago, when nothing like you was anywhere. Why should I care if you don't understand her?*

So Liz raised her arm and Fire took it as a signal. She lifted her wings and flew to a tree, and Liz took another dead chick from her pocket. Then she turned her back, held up her arm, and Fire slid down the sky toward her. A hawk! A modern dinosaur! Gorgeous, intense, and nothing like a person!

Liz could only watch in awe, knowing how much it would take to understand hawks. She would leave that to Gaia if Gaia was near, and keep coming to see Nancy Cowan.

Prologue

I am flying. The landscape slips and slides below as I bank into my turns. Around me I sense air currents moving and rising in the warmth of the sunny afternoon. Suddenly I am riding an accelerated elevator upward. As if pulled swiftly by a cable, I ascend higher, so high I am becoming part of the sky itself.

Apprehension pricks my consciousness and pulls me back to my earth-bound body. My hands fumble as I pull the lure from my pocket as fast as I can. I begin swinging it upwards at my side in a clockwise circle. I blow my whistle, although my hawk is now too high to hear it. She is steadily rising, following her first cartwheel into the capricious updraft that snagged her into an effortless, soaring ascension. She has never been so high above me. My mouth is dry; my heart is pounding. Will she see the lure? Will she respond to my enticement for her to drop from the heights and return?

She sees . . . *what* does she see? She sees the lure with a quarter of a quail carcass tied upon it. To her, the lure with its upward swing is prey. For my hawk, to catch prey is to live. Her dark silhouette is tiny and far away, but it changes to an arrow shape as she folds her wings and slips down through the atmosphere. She drops and weaves like a skier descending a steep slope. My breath is in time with the swing of the lure and all the while a part of my brain is calculating, calculating . . . timing the swing so at the final instant I can fling it skyward in precisely the angle to intercept the path of my raptor.

The lure flies from my outstretched hand and the action plays in slow motion as it meets my bird's descent. My hawk turns sideways as she passes the ascending object and her talons reach out. I hear the rap of those talons hitting the hard leather. Still descending, she swings upright and spreads her wings to slow herself as she rides the lure the last few feet to the ground. I run to join her and kneel beside where she, with mantled wings arched over her prize, begins to tear at the quail.

My hand searches beneath her outspread wings to take up each of her jesses, affixing them to the snap of the leash tied off to my glove while she is busy at the task of tearing morsels of meat. I take a deep breath. The heartbeat pounding in my ears is slowing now that the adrenaline rush is over. Slipping the fingers of my gloved left hand under the lure and holding her jesses in my right fist, I lift her as I stand. Aside from fluttering her wings to maintain her balance on the slippery leather, none of this unsettles my hawk. It is not until I leave the field carrying my bird that I am fully restored to my normal self: a person making her way home with a hawk riding her gloved hand. A car slows as I walk along the roadside. "Flying today?" my neighbor calls out with a smile.

"Yes," I reply, returning his smile. "I have been flying."

What is this spell that overcame me so I saw what the hawk saw, so I lived for a moment as she lives and flew with wings able to sense the invisible bumps and ruts of air currents rising? How have I become a partner with a creature weighing barely two pounds, whose brain can't remember what she saw just seconds ago but can recall a place she momentarily alighted upon years before? We are so different, the hawk and I. Yet we often function in complete unity; my mind is her mind, her body is my body. The bond between us is mystical, but is rooted in practical techniques handed down over countless generations.

I step from the road when I reach my driveway. Having eaten the quail quarter from the lure, my hawk is now sated. Her full crop is a rounded protrusion above her breastbone. Because of this she will not fly again today, and probably not tomorrow as well. I am recovering from the terrifying excitement of having my bird caught in a thermal updraft, a seductive, rising column of air that can carry my hawk in its power until she is beyond retrieval. The experience scared me nearly witless. Were it not for the training fostered upon me by nearly three decades of the practice of falconry, I could have lost her forever. But when the need came, I was prepared to do exactly the things necessary to draw my bird away from her aerial rapture.

The age-old methods did not fail me. My hawk responded as though she and I had planned it all out ahead of time. The ancient art has taught me to come to the field with something capable of exerting a pull upon her more powerful than the enchantment of the spiraling soar towards the heavens. Why else would a humble, floppy device of leather be so appropriately named "the lure"?

I reach her mew, pull open the door made of old barn-boards, and push aside the weighted canvas sheet hanging behind it to step inside. In the gloom of my bird's quarters, I unsnap the leash from her jesses. The hawk, having eaten all there was to eat, is done with me, with the lure and with my glove. She is as content as a creature such as she can be. She jumps to her high perch, then turns to watch me as I leave. She settles in for the evening as I exit, and I hear the jingle of the bell attached to her anklet.

From my kitchen window I can scan eight small buildings, two lines of four facing one another, standing along the edges of the field to the south. At the north side of the house, there are two more dwellings built into an old post-and-beam barn. Each of these habitations has bars at the window and a double door, and is kept securely locked. The individuals behind those padlocked entryways are not criminals or crazed psychopaths, but are partners with me and my husband at this old farm. All the security measures in place are for the protection of our valued friends within. The buildings and the barn house the four hawks and six falcons living here, but sometimes these feathered entities come inside to share our living quarters as intimately as we share our lives with them.

PART ONE

OWNED BY A HAWK

CHAPTER 1

A Different Way of Life

I enter her chamber like a lover, murmuring a silly song celebrating her beauty. She is a white gyrfalcon, the largest of her kind. In all of falconry's long history, pure white gyrfalcons have been prized. And she is sweet, which means she has no bad manners and is remarkably and uncharacteristically docile. As she first began to see, she has been cared for by human hands and looked up into human faces. Now, imprinted on humans, she sees me as one like herself. Grown to maturity, she views me as a mate. I must fulfill her expectations, must adopt the formalities of bonding with her to greet her in a manner ordained by her instincts. If I can do this, she will remain trusting and calm with me.

Never mind I am human and she is avian; she is imprinted on humans, after all. Never mind I am also female. She loves human females as much as a falcon can or does because a woman cared for her as her infant eyes became sighted. I am wooing this large, sweet, most beautiful falcon so I may become her mate. We can either be happily married or, if I fail abysmally in pleasing her, we can divorce and she will hate me. Her docility will evaporate the nearer I approach. Dealing with her will take on aspects of a battle. Handling an imprinted gyrfalcon who detests me is not something to which I aspire.

It may seem odd that I am avidly pursuing the mysteries of becoming wedded to a big white bird. After all, I have been happily married to my husband for many years. Although he will deny it, these cold, wintry hours I spend courting a gyrfalcon are his fault. She was his gift to me, just as is the life I lead now.

I fell in love when I was seventeen. He was handsome, a dashing Citadel cadet, like no one I had met before, and he drove my folks nuts. As if those admirable qualities were not enough, he spoke my language: animals. Back then, my life was filled with horses. A giveaway horse no one wanted had been offered to me years before. My mare became one of the best jumpers in the county and was joined in our barn by a second horse, an open jumper. At seventeen, I was a riding instructor earning the money for my horse expenses. Then I met the cadet who had grown up in New England and spent most of his free time in the forest before coming south to school. Jim was as animal-crazy as I was horse-crazy. He had raised raccoons and flying squirrels, and a hurt pigeon he hid from his parents in an antique rolltop desk. When he took me north to meet his family, his mom told me about the day she discovered the pigeon. We still have the desk, with pigeon peck marks inside the drawer where he kept the corn.

Soon after we met, Jim became a falconer. His adventures with training and keeping animals fascinated me. But keeping various species of wildlife was not allowed at a military college, which is why my parents ended up with a hawk in the garage. In short, Jim and I were meant for each other. To this day, over fifty years later, we marvel at our good fortune in finding one another. Had we married other people, we joke, we would have driven them insane.

My marriage to a man with an overwhelming love of nature and animals has led to a life on the wild side. Jim was nearing forty when he announced, "I want to get back into falconry." At the time, he seemed to me to be perilously close to doddering old age. "You better hurry up," I told him. "You haven't got much time.

After my husband's announcement, he soon discovered that we lived in a state where falconry was not included among the hunting laws. Until placed under regulation by the state, falconry could not be legal here. As a result, Jim initiated the bill leading New Hampshire to become the forty-sixth state in the United States to accept falconry. It was for Jim the resumption of a sport he had practiced years before.

When Jim said he wanted to get back into falconry, I supported him enthusiastically. As one of his Christmas presents, I promised to help him lobby for his falconry bill. By the time it became a law, I was calling my Christmas offer "the gift that keeps on giving." In other words, it took years to get his bill passed. It soon became clear I would need to learn more about falconry so I could effectively speak to politicians at hearings. Along the way I began to understand the new lifestyle my husband was embracing.

We sought acceptance of falconry by notifying the Audubon Society of New Hampshire (ASNH) about Jim's proposed legislation. Before long we were invited to a meeting with forty of its members and staff. Each of the forty was dedicated to his or her own vision of wild bird protection. Some at the table had misgivings about anyone they considered less knowledgeable than themselves becoming involved with the raptors in the state. Others were not in favor of hunting in any form. Jim calmly answered their questions. By the time the discussion ended, the air had warmed somewhat. While we had not won over everyone in the room, the ASNH told Jim they would not oppose our bill.

The next big hurdle would be dealing with the New Hampshire Fish and Game Department. Later when I thought back, facing the tension-filled Audubon meeting room was a cakewalk compared to my initial experience with the state agency.

I made an appointment with the acting director of the Fish and Game Department and the head of the game division to meet at their headquarters in Concord. My heart was set on making a good impression. Little did I know what I was in for. The "meeting" quickly devolved to something resembling an interrogation, but I strove to maintain the equilibrium and poise Jim had shown at Audubon. Things did not go well. The director and head of the game division derided falconry as an elitist activity. Finally they let me know the interview was over and dismissed me. Trembling from suppressed emotion, I walked to my car and promptly burst into tears, certain I had lost the cause of falconry in New Hampshire permanently. How could I face Jim with the news?

Jim took the news with perfect equanimity. He had a better understanding of the stonewalling techniques of government departments, so he set to work procuring all the information he could on falconry and how it was licensed in other states. In this, he had an ally in the North American Falconers Association (NAFA), of which he was a member. My role became one of relaying messages to and from Colonel Kent Carnie, NAFA's liaison for falconry legalization. Falconry-friendly state governments, environmental organizations supporting falconry, and regional falconry clubs were notified of our cause. Very soon manila envelopes full of documentation, laws and regulations from other states, conservationists' testimonials to the value of falconry, and reams of encyclopedic data began to arrive in our mailbox.

On the home front, our two state representatives were working for us. Betsy McKinney, the first rep to sign on in support of Jim's proposed legislation, made sure she and I attended every function where she could put our legislation before other legislators. Handshakes, greetings, quick "sound bites" about falconry became my stock in trade through her tutelage. My confidence in dealing with bureaucrats began to recover. Our other representative-sponsor, Bill Boucher, who was older and wiser, was incensed about what had happened to me at the Fish and Game

Department meeting. He aggressively worked the halls of the Legislative Office Building on our behalf.

After we were assigned a date for the hearing before the House Fish and Game Committee, we decided the best proposal to bring was a duplication of the Massachusetts falconry regulations. It was a forty-page document spelling out every possible activity involved with falconry. What could go wrong with such a game plan? Our state could simply follow the statutes and rules already adopted by our neighbor state.

As we filed into the hearing room, Jim put his name, as did Betsy and Bill, on the list of those who wished to speak. The state representatives of the committee were seated around conference tables arranged in a U-shape. At the podium, Betsy made a point of saying New Hampshire was so much a sportsmen's state, she had been shocked to find that an established form of hunting—falconry—was not a legal activity. The falconry bill was meant to remedy this abysmal oversight. Jim made his statement, and then it was time to hear from the opposition. Howie Nowell, the game division chief and one of the men who had confronted me in the meeting at Fish and Game headquarters, came forward to speak. "This is what they are bringing us!" Howie exclaimed, waving our forty-page bill aloft. "You have to have a dictionary to read it! Why, do you know that it allows for *imping* in this state?!"

The members of the Fish and Game Committee shifted uncomfortably in their chairs as they shared looks with one another. *Imping?! Here??* their faces said with revulsion, as if some kind of unspeakable deviance was involved. It didn't matter that none of them understood that "imping" is the falconry term for repairing broken feathers.

The falconry bill was voted "inexpedient to legislate." Jim and I were downcast. Betsy and Bill, however, were breezily unaffected. "Bring it back next year," Bill said.

"Nothing *ever* gets passed on the first go-round," Betsy consoled.

"There is too much inertia to overcome in state government the first time a bill is heard. Bring it back next year. We will help."

So we began the process again with more documents arriving in the mail, more meet-and-greets with representatives. After the first run at legislation, falconry began to have a presence throughout the halls of the state capitol building. When I attended legislative social events with Betsy, I found most of the representatives knew about our failed attempt and their curiosity was piqued. To get answers for the questions I was asked sometimes required leaving messages at a general store in the Arizona desert where Colonel Carnie and his friend Tom had gone to hunt with their falcons. Often it was Tom who called back to patiently supply me with the answers. Eventually I learned the falconer named Tom was Tom Cade, the founder of the Peregrine Fund.

The word of Jim's falconry bill spread throughout falconry circles in other states. We were invited to tour mews (raptor living quarters) in Massachusetts so Jim could plan his own. There he met a master falconer who worked nights at a factory so he could fly falcons during the day. The master invited Jim down to go out with him flying his falcon. This man agreed to serve as Jim's sponsor when the day came he could be licensed. On one of the trips to visit Jim's sponsor, who was also a breeder of falcons, I went along. As Jim and the master falconer talked, I watched in fascination as a pair of mated prairie falcons exchanged nest-sitting duties within the breeding quarters situated in the man's backyard.

The Maine falconers extended invitations for us to join them when they flew their birds. We were quick to take up these friendly overtures, and so one day found ourselves in Maine watching a young woman fly her newly trained goshawk on pheasant. After retrieving her hawk, the falconer, still in her teens, told us how she had spent many hours with her young gos, nearly all day of every day, as she raised it from a downy nestling to be a calm and steady hunting partner.

Following the pheasant hunt, we drove in a convoy to the Saco Marsh, a low-lying area near the coast of Maine. The plan was to fly falcons there. Those of us who came to watch, learn, or just follow along were instructed to fan out and run across the marsh in order to flush birds into the air. The last instruction was a warning: "The falcons are just getting back into the air after being laid up for the summer molt. They might not fly high, and they might be tempted to stoop on whichever of you is standing the tallest."

What did *that* mean? Stooping on whoever is tallest? I was one of the shortest people there, but I did not want to be left "standing tall" when the others were bent to avoid a head-on collision with a large, sharp-taloned raptor! Jim and I found ourselves running and leaping over water-filled ditches, all the while bent over at the waist. It was hard work and I was soon out of breath. Bent at the waist, hands on my knees, I raised my head and looked around.

Saco Marsh is shaped like a large, round bowl. Beyond the marsh edge, a highway circled the perimeter. Cars were pulling over onto the shoulder of the road, and people were getting out and watching. Some had binoculars trained on us. I wondered if they had any idea what on earth these bent-over people were doing out in the middle of the marsh. Then a police car pulled over and the officer trained *his* binoculars on us. Despite my consternation at looking like an idiot, we did not get arrested.

At the end of the day we were dead-tired, but we had made many friends who loyally showed up at our next hearing to support our bill and again at our house to help work out the regulations. Jim and I talked all the way home about how exciting it was to watch the goshawk in pursuit of game and to have falcons flying overhead. Despite whatever we had looked like as we ran hither and yon shouting "Ho! Hawk!" it had been a very good day.

When it came closer to time to file again, we knew our initial bill needed some adjusting. Jim contacted the Fish and Game Department this time, and found things had changed there. The acting director who had persecuted me during my meeting the year before had retired. There was a new director named Alan Crabtree, who spoke to Jim. He genially invited Jim to meet him at headquarters to talk over our move to bring falconry to the state. Jim and I went to see him.

We discovered that New Hampshire's Fish and Game Department had been stuck in the past for a long time. The department was composed of two divisions: fish and game. And that was it. There was nothing in the department that served the environment or threatened or endangered species. Luckily for us, Alan wanted New Hampshire Fish and Game to provide for *all* wildlife, not just creatures that could be hunted, trapped, or caught on fishhooks.

Alan asked us a few questions and gave thoughtful answers to what we asked him. He studied us throughout the interview and no doubt saw a fairly average couple who would be persistent about their reasonable request to have New Hampshire adopt falconry as a legal means of hunting. While he made us no promises, he told us he would be back in touch very soon.

In our next conversation with Alan, he propositioned us. "Would you consider," he asked, "changing your falconry bill to read that the funds from licensing would be held in an account used to provide conservation measures for the state's raptors? You will have one hundred percent backing from Fish and Game, and your falconry bill will be New Hampshire's first non-game beneficial legislation." Jim quickly agreed with Alan's plan, and when he told the North American Falconers Association about the new and improved falconry proposal, it easily won the endorsement and approval from that quarter as well.

In the meantime, the Fish and Game Department told Jim he could go ahead with his falconry career by obtaining a license in another state and that he could keep a hawk in New Hampshire as long as he did not hunt with it here until his bill had become law. Jim's sponsor was the Massachusetts falconer, and he took his test in Maine to obtain a falconry license from that state. Maine sent the paperwork off to the federal office for cosigning and sending back to Jim. He waited patiently for his federal falconry permit to come back from the United States Fish and Wildlife Service (USFWS) permits office, and waited, and waited.

Whether it was a bureaucratic snafu or unintentional ineptitude, the office said it "lost" his paperwork three times. This left Jim a licensed, but birdless, falconer. By the time he finally received the license, trapping season for falconry raptors had ended in Maine. Jim contacted Tom Early, the Massachusetts Division of Fisheries and Wildlife falconry coordinator, to learn if he could trap a hawk in that state. Instead, Tom arranged for Jim to pick up a young red-tailed hawk that was due to be released back to the wild from Tufts Wildlife Clinic.

When we went to Tufts to pick one out of three juvenile red-tails, Jim had to make a decision. Two of the birds were in rehab at the clinic due to injuries in which each had lost an eye. The third young red-tail had been picked up in a backyard when it landed on a squirrel shot by the homeowner. This young bird had been too debilitated from an internal parasitic infestation to fly away, but now it was strong and healthy again. "I don't think that bird will make a good falconry bird," Tom told Jim. "It is a very high-strung bird and will take a lot of work to calm down." While we were still working to get Jim's bill passed, we knew it would be unwise to bring a one-eyed red-tailed hawk back to New Hampshire, as Howie Nowell, the game division chief, had made it clear he felt any raptor so damaged should be euthanized. Thus, Jim chose the two-eyed, high-strung red-tail to bring home from the Tufts Wildlife Clinic flight cage.

Jim brought his young red-tail home, promptly naming it Tabasco, and then something incredible happened. I was standing on the deck of our split-level house watching Jim as he entered Tabasco's mew, emerging with his hawk on his glove. Understanding the intricacies of falconry equipment is something apprentices must master, and Jim hadn't handled a raptor in a long time. As he left the mew, he had the leash wrapped loosely about his glove. Falconry leashes have two very different ends. One end is just that—the *end* of the leather strap. The opposite end has a leather button, which is usually the leash folded back and forth and then passed through a slit in itself, so this bulky "button" is a block to passing through the circlet of the swivel joining the leash to the jesses. Grab the wrong end of the leash, and the non-button end smoothly plays out through the swivel. Suddenly, the bird is no longer attached to the falconer.

That is what happened to Jim. With horror, I watched as Tabasco flapped his wings and took off to where my sled dogs were quartered. It landed on a doghouse, where it found itself nearly nose to nose with my smallest husky. None of us moved or breathed, not even the husky. The hawk suddenly realizing it was in a very precarious position, took off and landed on a pine bough directly above Jim's head. Jim reached up, took up the bird's jesses, and Tabasco jumped to his glove. My heart resumed beating in my chest. Since the hawk had been with us only a day or two and was not trained or used to Jim, neither of us could quite believe what had just occurred, but you can bet my husband never allowed something like that to happen again. Not ever.

The falconry bill passed the house and senate overwhelmingly. A month or so later, the governor finally signed our falconry bill into falconry law after three very intense years of lobbying and legislating.

CHAPTER 2

I Begin

I have to do this right, I say to myself as my brain reviews the procedures and I slip a heavy leather glove onto my left hand. I am quaking inside, knowing in falconry one seldom gets a second chance if a mistake is made. With the other hand I turn the lock, open the hasp, and swing the creaking door outwards. Slipping past the canvas sheet over the interior of the doorway, I quietly enter the shed.

The inhabitant is waiting for me. He turns his cold, implacable countenance to face me. Standing in shadow, I bait my glove with the sleight-of-hand dexterity of a magician, then step forward to present a dead day-old chick. Immediately there is a *ka-thump* of two pounds of muscle and bone wrapped in a formidable mass of feathers which is now sitting upon my leather-covered wrist, inches from my jawline. The chick disappears in fast and greedy fashion as the hawk devours it, ripping it to pieces during the process. Day-old chickens live off the yoke of the egg from which they hatched, making this chick a veritable "yoke bomb."

Finished, the raptor gives his head a shake. Yellow droplets of yolk fly past my face. Some of the dribble lands on my chin. I am a mixture of emotions, my shirt as well as my chin bearing evidence of the raptor's savage feast. I am compelled to feed this feathered monster with talons sharp and strong enough to remove my fingers because I am determined to be a falconer. My mission now is to get a second chick onto the glove exactly where this raptor is sitting. The longer I consider this, the larger the bird grows in my vision until he is a giant. The hawk knows he holds the advantage. My associate-of-the-glove sends a look my way that plainly says, "N-n-n-n-e-e-x-x-t!"

How could anyone relate to a creature as cold and emotionless as a bird of prey? But I had watched with interest the developing partnership between my husband and his red-tailed hawk. Despite this, I was in no way prepared to make a commitment to a raptor. To become licensed is a lot of work and involves passing a written test. I would need a sponsor, an experienced falconer willing to help me with no remuneration other than a sense of sportsmanship. The closest falconer to me had volunteered to serve as my sponsor once he became a general-level falconer. But being sponsored by, taking orders from, *my husband*?! I was not ready to go there, yet.

Another requirement for the falconry license was to have a hunting license. I had never hunted a day in my life. To obtain a hunting license meant taking a six-week-long course with a volunteer group of hunter education instructors in another town. Becoming a licensed falconer seemed much more difficult a task than I wanted to undertake, but the relationship between Jim and his hawk was exerting a pull I could no longer deny. I *had* to learn more about this intriguing association with a bird which had taken over my husband.

One of the things Jim does when training a hawk is to walk out with it on his glove. Sitting close to his body, hearing his voice, seeing his movements, and learning to balance to the cadence of his steps all serve to accustom a raptor to its falconer. Jim walked a lot with Tabasco, and because hiking the trails had often been a source of shared fun and exercise, I went along. Our Siberian husky / German shepherd cross, Inga, would come as well.

Jim's hawk became accustomed to both of us humans and the dog as we hiked for miles, from the wooded logging road behind our subdivision to the trail along the power lines and into, around, and through the conservation area of Londonderry known as the Musquash. Despite living in a part of the state that was beginning to explode with growth, we knew we would cross paths with some form of wildlife as we hiked through this important north–south wildlife corridor. We soon learned if Jim's hawk turned his head to stare in a particular direction, we should look there, too, to see what he had spotted. Traveling with a raptor was a revelation to what we might not have seen otherwise.

On one hike a coyote as large as Inga kept pace with us as we walked the power lines, trotting only a few yards within the cover of the forest. Another day we spooked up a mother moose and her calf. Wild hawk sightings became frequent occurrences. The hawks, instead of flying away, were coming nearer to see Jim's hawk. They were obviously curious about what another hawk was doing in their area. One day as we crossed a field, a female red-tailed hawk flew directly towards us and circled at a low altitude before lazily flying back to the woods. Minutes later, her mate did a flyover. I wondered if the two had been sitting observing us, or if the hen hawk told her mate about the strange sight of one of their kind being accompanied by two humans and a dog.

Another raptor encounter was more spectacular. We had entered the Musquash conservation area by means of a narrow path, arriving at an old road which divided a pond with a beaver dam on one end and a heron rookery on the other. Young ATV riders were roaring back and forth as we neared the road. Beyond the heron rookery was the Londonderry Fish and Game Club, from which emanated the sound of rifle shots. Jim and I elected to avoid the noisy ATV traffic, so we crossed carefully over the top of the beaver dam to a path winding around a hill beside the pond. To top this, a passenger jet overhead began its descent to Manchester Airport. Suddenly an osprey dove into the pond with a splash, and emerged with a wriggling fish in its talons. With all the noise from the ATVs, the gunfire, and the large jet, not to mention a fish dinner in its talons, I expected the osprey would have more on its agenda than to spy on two humans, a dog, and a hawk, but I was wrong. As soon as the osprey saw our entourage, he hovered above us to get a good look at what this other raptor was doing in his territory.

The more time I spent with Jim as he worked with his bird, the more I felt an urge to join in this strange and new adventure of being a falconer. When the hunter education course was offered again, I signed up to take it. In January 1990 I passed the falconry exam, applied for my state and federal falconry licenses, and began my apprenticeship with Jim.

Jim was now working with his first falcon. I began my apprenticeship with Tabasco instead of trapping a young bird, as at the time, our state allowed this. However, I was timid about insinuating myself into the solid partnership between Jim and this hawk. Tabasco sensed my hesitancy and took advantage of it. For the first few months, the hawk had me over a barrel. Whenever he stomped on my glove and glared at me, I provided food. He had the upper hand due to my lack of experience until the day I recognized as a sham the threatening performance he gave. My timidity vanished, though my relationship with Tabasco never matched the intensity of the one he shared with Jim. Working with him taught me the rudiments, but I did not strive to go further as I would have with a hawk I had trained myself.

After apprenticing, a falconer typically moves to the "general" level and may possess two birds and move beyond to other species of raptors. As I ended my apprenticeship with Jim, I was excited about getting a second hawk, one to train by myself. Jim and I read about Harris's hawks and how companionable, dependable, and loyal they are. Females were reputed to be calmer and are larger than males, as is true of all raptors. I became convinced training a female Harris's hawk would enable me to progress in falconry. I did not know then that my connection with this creature would be more intense than any I'd experienced with an animal. My life was about to be radically altered.

CHAPTER 3

Meeting Injun

Acquiring the new bird was the result of a chance meeting at a gun show, when Jim was stopped by a man who noted the North American Falconers Association patch on his jacket. Both men were falconers, had grown up a few miles apart in Worcester, Massachusetts, and shared an interest in antique weaponry. When Jim returned to the car, he told me about the encounter. "His name is Tom Ricardi. When I mentioned you were a falconer, too, and were looking for a Harris's hawk, he said he had a young one he was looking to give to a good home. Too bad it is a male. I told him you wanted a female."

"What?!" I exclaimed. "I don't care if it is a male. I want it anyway!"

That same week, we found our way down to Tom's home in western Massachusetts.

"The bird is four months old," Tom said to us. "I got him because the first Harris's I got, his older sister, did not seem to be catching on to hunting, but now she has begun to do really well. I have, consequently, not done anything with this young bird at all, and if he does not start training soon, he may get sour and be harder for someone to take over." The young male was so wild, Tom had to throw a towel over him as he flew by. The intent was to slow the bird down just enough so Tom could grab one of its legs, but the bird crashed into the wall and fell into a heap on the floor. When Tom scooped him up, he was one mad bird!

Together, the three of us worked at outfitting the young Harris's with anklets and jesses. Tom slipped my swivel through the slits of the jesses, ran my leash through the other circlet on the swivel, and handed the bird to me. As he did so, one long, slender leg snatched out at me. There was not a doubt of the meaning there. I got the youngster upright on my glove, where he glared at me and let out a harsh scream. "He hasn't seen women before, Nancy," Tom said. "He will get used to you, don't worry."

By the time we reached home it was late in the day, but the next morning, bright and early, the first order of business was to start training my new hawk. The initial step was to convince him I was not a monster who ate young hawks. Maddeningly, the hawk was much calmer around my husband. Raptors are very observant. They take note of each tiny difference from details with which they are familiar. If men are all they have seen up close in their short lives, rather than recognizing a woman as the female variety of "human," women are perceived as frightening "other creatures."

I had a perch set up on a tarp in our living room, and I sat for hours in front of the young bird with a dead chick on my glove. The first day passed with no luck. This hawk was having no part of me. He made this very clear by flying or bating off the perch in an effort to get away from me as I sat before him. Since he was tethered to the perch, he did not get far, and because raptors have an instinct to head for the higher perch, he would return to sit while glaring suspiciously at me and the food I offered.

Day one passed in this fashion. Day two was much the same. By the beginning of day three, however, we were making progress. Now the hawk was tired (he was not the only one) and would lean towards the fresh chick on my glove and smack his lips. Actually, hawks don't have lips, but when they open and close their beaks while gazing longingly at the food, the action is exactly like a person smacking his lips. As the hawk leaned towards the chick, he very nearly stepped from the perch to my glove just a few inches away. I kept the chick close enough to tempt him, but far enough away so he couldn't quite reach it no matter how far he leaned. This game went on for the next two hours.

About halfway through day three, it was clear the stalemate would end very soon. The hawk was leaning so close to the food on my glove, he was almost to the point of falling off his perch. All this time, I was staying as still as a statue. Any move, any turn of my head, and he would immediately back off. I was just too much of an unfamiliar "alien-being" for him to relax in my proximity. Jim watched our battle of wills with interest. His movements around me and the hawk did not startle the bird as much as did any slight motion from me. Every muscle was rebelling against the position I had assumed. And now Nature was calling. I finally put the chick leg down and made a hasty exit for the bathroom.

When I returned a few moments later, the leg was missing. My husband was standing near the hawk with a big smile. "He came to the glove for the chick leg," Jim said. "I am sure it will not be long before he comes to you, too."

Hell hath no greater fury than a woman who endured two and a half days with a stubborn hawk, only to have her husband entice the bird to the glove the moment she leaves the room. I was so angry, I could have beaten Jim senseless. In the interest of self-preservation, he fled the room. An hour or so later, my hawk finally made a step to *my* gloved hand. Jim was sincere and hearty with his congratulations and his praise (as well he should have been!), and my wounded feelings were overwhelmed by my excitement at moving ahead with training.

By the end of the day, the hawk had consumed numerous chick pieces while on my glove and had settled down enough to stay there. Every day we tried some variation, which included longer jumps to the glove and going out-of-doors to start the jump-to-the-glove process again in wide, open spaces. Next was what Jim had done with his red-tail, taking long walks while the bird rode my glove. The more time spent with me, the more things he saw while on the glove, the more dinners consumed in peace after his jump to my hand, the more the hawk began to trust me. By the end of three weeks, I reached the breathless moment of setting my bird free. His speedy return on my whistle made my head spin with relief and happiness.

Once trained, the hawk and I began to get to know each other. I was delighted with every flight. When I called him to the glove, he swooped in to hit it solidly and powerfully. I marveled over the red of his shoulders, the leg feathers colored like cinnamon and sugar, the deep chocolate shade of his back. Harris's hawks are native to the American Southwest and parts of Mexico. I imagined if an Aztec of long ago had painted a mural of a hawk, it would have looked like this bird. I picked a name for him, and later, when people suggested to me it was politically incorrect, I was surprised. I felt only respect for my raptor, and would never have given him a name I felt was disrespectful to anyone. This hawk was proud, beautiful, the combination of an independent spirit and wildness. I thought the name"Injun" suited him perfectly.

CHAPTER 4

The Attack and the Mission

Expectancy mingled with the cold air of the January woods behind our house. A shout rose from my husband, unseen in the denseness of the woodlot, as a flying quail suddenly appeared in the clearing ahead. My young hawk bolted from my glove like a missile, almost too fast for my eyes to follow. But I saw the quail. *Poof!* The bird exploded in a cloud of buff, russet, and dark brown feathers and disappeared. I ran to the location of this make-the-quail-disappear act to find Injun, his dark wings mantled over the fallen leaves, the deceased quail clutched in his talons. Injun raised his head from his kill, his beak red and dripping with blood, and glared at me with eyes as hard and cold as diamonds.

So far the winter had been fairly mild. It was important to cement our new partnership in falconry by starting Injun at hunting as soon as possible. His first chance on quail ended with a superb flight and a swift kill that belied his inexperience. Those solid, powerful hits to the glove had foretold he would perform well at hunting. According to the language of falconry, Injun was now "entered," which means that his hunting career had begun.

Further hunting excursions were cut short by bad weather, at the end of which I returned to flying Injun to the glove from various perches, omitting any hunting opportunities. Then something bewildering happened one day a week or so later. After flying, I returned Injun to his mew, to have him perch quietly while I removed his jesses. It was a companionable time I enjoyed now that Injun and I were supposedly becoming friends. But Injun did something entirely unexpected after I removed one of the jesses. He reached over with his free foot and wrapped his talons around my bare wrist. He was not hurting me, but I was firmly imprisoned in his grasp. (I was to learn later, from another falconer, that the term for this is "braceletting.") I was wearing a handcuff of talons and toes. Time stood still as he held my wrist and gazed at me strangely. Then in a flash, he stared at me as though I was a total stranger or his most hated enemy and let out a raucous scream. The episode passed as swiftly as it had come, and Injun released my hand. I left the mew wondering what on earth I had just witnessed.

A few days later, I got that look again and another scream. This time Injun's open, taloned foot rapped my face and left a small puncture wound on my cheek. Within moments, Injun was back to his old self. I could not imagine what was causing this strange behavior.

Some days afterward, as I was changing Injun's flight jesses, I found him once again fixing me with an odd, hostile stare. He screamed and, as he did, his free foot came up to hit me a hard blow in the face. It felt as if someone had punched me in the mouth. Almost immediately his gaze returned to normal and the moment passed, but I knew I had sustained some damage. Injun had punched me between my nose and mouth with his razor-sharp talons. By the time I had finished with his jesses and had Injun tethered to a perch, my hands were covered with blood streaming down from my face.

I went to the bathroom to clean up. A wave of dizziness came over me when I saw myself in the mirror. From one nostril and down to the top of my upper lip, the skin was laid open in a deep, slicing gash. Blood covered my chin entirely in scarlet and poured down my neck to drip across the front of my shirt. I ran warm water from the tap and with a washcloth gingerly cleaned the sticky mess from my face and throat. The stream of crimson had coagulated so the wound was no longer bleeding, but even with the blood cleaned away, the wound was ugly, with swollen edges of the gash making it appear even deeper than it was. It was mean-looking evidence of an attack. I had no clue what had provoked Injun to attack me, but I had to find out. I would not be able to safely handle and fly this bird of which I had grown so fond unless I did.

The first person I consulted was, of course, my husband. Jim had no more experience with Harris's hawks than did I, but he knew a good hawk when he saw one and did not want anything to deter me from continuing to work with Injun. "Just keep on like it did not happen, and it will probably work itself out" was his advice. Like me, he had read all the literature touting Harris's as companionable, cooperative, friendly partners.

I was not willing to take this advice and told him so. What I had experienced was certainly not companionable or friendly. If an attack came again, would it cost me an eye?

The next person I spoke with was a supplier of falconry equipment out on the West Coast. I knew he had recently gotten a Harris's, a female, so when I called him with an order, I told him of my experience. He was surprised, as he had not had any similar occurrence with his bird. "I will think of you now, Nancy," he said, "as the person with the face-killing Harris's hawk!"

I was not amused by his comment.

"Why don't you call Ken Felix?" Jim suggested. This was an excellent idea. Ken had flown a Harris's for years. He was president of the North American Falconers Association as well, and a practicing veterinarian who served as the consulting vet for both the Philadelphia Zoo and the Commonwealth of Pennsylvania.

Ken listened carefully to my story of the braceletting and the attacks. "Gee, Nancy, I just don't know why this happened. And I bet your bird doesn't know either. But I also bet he is as sorry about it as you are."

I told Ken, with all due respect, that I agreed Injun did not understand why he had attacked me. The attacks had come out of nowhere and disappeared just as quickly. But I could not agree Injun was sorry about it. I was not even sure he remembered it. Ken, like my husband, urged me to keep on with the bird as though nothing had happened. I hung up thinking perhaps I had accepted a male too quickly. Like our equipment supplier, Ken flew a female Harris's. Maybe female Harris's hawks were the kinder, gentler, more cooperative sex after all.

Another falconer kindly offered to take Injun off my hands. Despite the conviviality, I prickled at his words. I was not about to give up my bird! And I was not frightened of Injun—just wary and not wanting to lose an eye ... or two.

I did not let the attacks keep me from flying Injun, but I was on guard every second. This hampered the enjoyment I normally got from working with him. I decided to try putting Injun in a spot where he was uneasy whenever I had to change his equipment. We happened to have an antique merry-go-round horse in our den. Injun didn't trust the wooden horse at all and kept himself busy glaring at it. This gained me some small measure of safety, but I couldn't take a merry-go-round horse with me to every place I went with the hawk. I needed to get to the bottom of matters as soon as possible. Jim and I talked it over. I stressed to him that unless I was protected in some way, I had no confidence in flying this bird.

"Frank Beebe has developed a new kind of glove with a pin or something you can hook into the jesses. Maybe a special glove like that would help you," Jim suggested one day. "You should call him."

Asking Frank Beebe for advice about hawks was like asking Moses for advice about the Ten Commandments. I had never met Frank, who lived in Vancouver, British Columbia. Beebe and Hal Webster collaborated on writing *North American Falconry and Hunting Hawks*, a work affectionately referred to by the majority of American falconers as "the Bible." He was more than a master of masters in the realm of falconry—he *was* Moses. But I was a desperate woman, so I called him.

I have never met or spoken with another falconer who would not, at the drop of a hat, stop whatever he's doing to help out a fellow falconer. It is inherent to the sport and to the passion of being a falconer. Frank was no different. He patiently listened to my tale of the events leading up to and including the attack. There was a pause after I finished, and then Frank began speaking. His words came slowly, and I knew he was giving serious consideration to my situation and to what he was telling me. "You know, there is a lot that has been written about Harris's hawks lately, and most of what is in print is crap." Frank explained that the words "cooperative" and "friendly" were poor attempts to describe attributes of a bird driven by instinct to do exactly what the person wanted it to do (hunting).

"Those little males, especially—there is a lot more going on with those birds than people realize," he said. "And if the falconers flying them don't pay attention, they'll end up with some problems." He told me male Harris's hawks were high-strung birds exhibiting a lot more hunting drive and aggression than new owners of Harris's were prepared to handle. He predicted more occurrences of what I had experienced would happen with others. Frank's next words were the most valuable gift he could have given me. "You will work out in time what caused the bird to strike out at you, but what you really want to know right now is how to fly the son-of-a-gun without getting hurt."

I murmured my assent. Frank had read my situation perfectly. He understood where I was at this point in time, and his final words to me were emphatically practical. "Well, just hold the little bastard's feet down so he can't get you!"

I developed for my own use what I refer to as the "Harris's Hawk Death Grip." I had begun falconry by emulating photos of accomplished falconers holding lovely, quiet birds regally on their hands with their jesses and leash draped artfully over and around the fingers of the glove. My grip gets right to the point of things. Both jesses are tucked snugly between the thumb and forefinger of my glove with little play for foot movement on the glove. The grip Frank had advised me to use enabled me to go onward with Injun, as Jim and Ken had suggested, as though nothing had happened. This was fine with Injun, who seemed to have no recollection of any of the events.

Frank's words had done more than give me a new grip and more confidence. As a result of what he told me, I was on a mission. I was flying now, but flying was no longer enough. I had to know what was going on inside Injun. I needed to understand what I had done or not done to instigate this behavior. My husband, with his voracious appetite for reading and collecting books on falconry, and his near photographic memory, were huge assets in the undertaking of enlightenment.

The first thing I had to do was to assess what had changed in Injun's world that may have affected his behavior. It did not take long for something to occur to me, and it was what should have been obvious all along, which was the fact he had been flown on prey. I found that it also helped to compare Injun to another hawk known for its strong hunting drive: the goshawk. Jim introduced me to the term "yarak" from one of his books. Despite differences in opinion, yarak is thought to mean a buildup of hunting aggression that causes the raptor to strike out without warning.

When we entered Injun on game, we had awakened his hunting instinct. Later, I came to realize raptors mature not by time but by *events*. Catching the quail had matured Injun and changed him from a young Harris's into a grown-up, hunting Harris's. Injun's hunting drive went into gear, and, just as suddenly, all this hunting energy became something the hawk could not control. It was not viciousness or meanness; rather it was like steam escaping from a pressure valve into the atmosphere.

Was there another way to release this pent-up energy? I wondered. I found my answer in the lure. Catching it (the more chasing that had to be done, the better) was a fair substitute for hunting, I discovered. While hunting with the bird was the optimum release for his drive, catching a lure could alleviate the buildup of the tension inside Injun. I could not run fast enough to make a challenge of catching the bunny lure, which is dragged on the ground, so my answer was to work my hawk on the bird or flying lure (which is swung through the air). I sought ways in which to swing it to make it harder to catch. Varying the speed and changing the orbit were two ways to increase the difficulty.

I learned as many tricks as I could to play "keep-away" so Injun found it challenging. And the more we "played," the better Injun got at catching it until he reached a point of such agility and speed that I could not get in more than one or two passes before he caught the lure out of the sky. Usually if hawks miss the lure, they will take a perch to swoop down once again on prey. Injun soon became so physically fit that if he missed a pass, he could turn in the air and re-pass again without stopping to perch in between. I got to be a much better lure swinger as a result of our workouts. We were now more in tune with one another and had found a way to keep Injun's yarak satisfactorily, if temporarily, squelched.

Besides alleviating my problem with Injun's levels of yarak, learning what made this fascinating bundle of nerves and instincts "tick" was as exciting as flying with him. I was ready to begin creating a partnership with my hawk.

CHAPTER 5

Compatibility on Injun's Terms

Injun and I flew every chance and every place we could. Our partnership had become a tangible thing, and I reveled in the intensity of it. Then summer came and I put my bird up, as we do when our raptors begin molting. "Putting up" falconry birds means they are not flown, but left in the mew or the weathering yard (an outdoor fenced-in area where birds can be left safely tethered to a perch) to enjoy a life of leisure. Feathers are lost over a period of time during which falconers feed their birds well to ensure the incoming feathers will be strong. Because the molting birds are overweight, they must be brought back to flying weight when the molt is done and flying season approaches. We then put our birds on a regimen of less food to bring their weight back down, and that's what I did with Injun.

As sometimes happens, he did not complete his full molt and had kept some of his juvenile tail feathers, but the beautiful cinnamon-and-sugar leg feathers I had so admired had been replaced with adult leggings matching the red patches on his shoulders. I was looking forward to the day he would begin to show avidity for food and we could again begin flights.

One afternoon I went out to feed him in the weathering yard. The fencing also covers overhead to protect the bird from the aerial attack of another bird or animal. On this day, Injun was sporting an enormously distended crop. He was so full of whatever he had eaten, the skin over his crop peeked grotesquely through his feathers. I could not imagine what he had consumed until I found the tail of a young chipmunk on the ground beside his perch. In whatever way the chippie had found his way into the weathering area, it was definitely a one-way trip. Plans for flying Injun had to wait a bit until he had digested his "chipmunk alfresco."

As time went on, things between Injun and me kept getting better and better. During each flight we took together, it seemed as though our hearts and minds belonged to a single entity. That fall we were asked to do a falconry presentation for a children's science museum. Jim and I had done talks for various groups before, and this was something I wanted to expand upon. It was fun to explain what I loved about our hawks and falcons, and people always seemed to appreciate learning more about the birds.

Tom Ricardi, who had given Injun to me, had become a close friend. Tom owned a large rehabilitation center for birds of prey. To help support it, he did innumerable talks for conservation groups and schools. I asked Tom about his presentations, knowing he sometimes included flight demonstrations. While he told me about his experiences flying Injun's sister, a plan began to form in my brain. When the day drew near, I told Jim I wanted to include a flight with Injun as part of my presentation. Jim was not enthused; he would rather have tested this before doing it "live" in front of an audience. I thought about an old adage I had learned when I was jumping horses: At the point of doing it, you must throw your heart over the jump first and hope for the rest to follow. I was counting on all the hours Injun and I had spent hunting and lure flying to enable my plan.

All things considered, I had butterflies in my stomach when the time came for the flight demonstration. Jim, Injun, and I went out to the yard behind the small museum building, followed by about fifty people. A big oak tree dominated one corner of the yard. When I cast Injun off my glove, he sailed up into the tree. As soon as I could wrap my shaking fingers around the chick leg in my pocket, I transferred it to my glove and blew the whistle. In a flash, Injun glided down from his high perch and the crowd exclaimed "Ahhh!" His first flight steadied my nerves, so we went on with several flights. Everything went as smoothly as if we were flying at home. Afterwards, members of the audience told us that seeing flight up close was an unforgettable end to a program they had enjoyed very much. This was the beginning of many years of flight demonstrations in front of thousands of people.

Injun may have been my partner, but he was no pussycat. His long-term memory and hair-trigger temper required that Jim do the coping, or beak shaping, while I held Injun on my glove. We cope the beaks of our birds because they are not at liberty, as are wild raptors, to find a carcass on which to tyre or nibble bits of flesh from large bones. This nibbling or tyring wears the beak to keep it properly shaped. I would hold Injun firmly on my glove during the process as Jim was treated to Injun giving a harsh scream and attempting to lunge at him. Injun would harbor his ill will against my husband for two weeks afterwards.

We had evidence this hawk could hold a grudge for even longer. The day Tom Ricardi caught Injun in the mew had resulted in an abrasion to his cere (which is the nostril area above the beak) when he collided with the wall. Injun seemed to blame Tom for this for the rest of his life. About two years after Tom had given the hawk to me, he came to our home to attend a gun show with Jim. I was anxious to show Injun off, so I asked Tom to come out to the mew. We had gotten only halfway across the yard before Injun sighted Tom and let out a horrid scream. "Same to you, you old son-of-a-B!" Tom hollered right back. I had wondered why

Injun would become sharp set, which means his posture showed him ready to launch himself towards and scream at mustached gentlemen wearing bill caps who attended our programs. After remembering that Tom had a mustache and often wore a bill cap, I now knew the reason. Even eight long years later, when we asked Tom to look over an injury Injun had sustained from a pheasant kick, Injun's reaction to him was exactly the same.

Fortunately Injun didn't carry a grudge towards me. In fact, he eventually became so trusting of me that I could do the beak coping myself. He would tolerate me while I held his beak with one hand and trimmed off the tip with my other hand. He seemed to be resigned to the necessity of the procedure. At the same time, Injun was never hesitant about letting me know if I had transgressed, no matter how innocent or unintentional the transgression had been.

One early spring day, when the weather was tempting us out-of-doors, Jim proposed a hike out at Camp Morgan, now a town park, in Washington, New Hampshire, where he had spent his youth as a counselor. For the first time in months, the sun was strong, and the snow covering the trails was finally melting. As was our custom, we each brought a raptor to carry along on the hike. We parked at Camp Morgan, where Jim unloaded his prairie falcon, Tater, while I lifted Injun out from his giant hood, tying his leash to my glove.

We started out along the old trail around Millen Pond as Jim pointed to where various camp buildings had once stood. The trail led into the woods and along the steep slope dropping down to the pond. Ahead of us we could hear the roaring of a boisterous cascade. To continue we had to cross a puncheon log bridge, which was built out of logs split lengthwise with their flat centers facing up in order to keep hikers from getting wet. On this day, however, the stream had grown from a trickle to a roaring torrent due to the snowmelt, and water occasionally splashed the walking surface of the logs.

As sure-footed as an antelope, Jim made a quick crossing carrying Tater and then turned to encourage me to follow. "Come ahead," he called out. "It's okay."

I stepped out to find that the bridge was indeed sturdy. But what I also learned was that the soles of my fashionable hiking footgear were disinclined to adhere to water-soaked logs. I slipped and flew into the air, tossing Injun from my glove to the bank near where Jim was waiting. My landing left me in a dilemma. My lower body had landed on the bridge and was still relatively dry. My upper half, however, was hanging upside down below the bridge. Moreover, I was *stuck*! My right elbow was wedged between two of the boulders in the stream. The full force of the water in my face was not at all pleasant. At least I was able to twist my torso and neck to see Jim, Tater, and Injun on the bank on the other side of the bridge. Sitting high and dry on the bank, Injun glared at me then let out a scream that seemed to say, *How dare you toss me aside so carelessly!*

My husband had Tater on his glove and was busy trying to keep Injun from tangling his leash, which was still attached to me. He had no spare hand to extricate me from my predicament. The only way out of the situation was for my bottom half to become as wet and as cold as my top half. Resignedly, I rolled my legs off the bridge. Once right side up, I was able to extricate my elbow. With the rushing water nearly knocking me off my feet, I clambered up the bank and onto the path. I was thoroughly soaked and very cold. Jim was anxious to return to the car to get me warmed up, so I once again had to cross the damn bridge while wearing the damn boots! I retrieved Injun to my glove, where he treated me to another scream as if I had misunderstood him the first time. Once across, it was a long, cold ride back to Londonderry. After a couple of days, and several good meals, Injun forgave me.

CHAPTER 6

Goshawk in the Bedroom

As Injun and I continued building our relationship, Jim was moving ahead with his own falconry ambitions and dreams by acquiring the tiercel (male) goshawk he named Cadet. Once a falconer has become a general falconer, he is allowed by law to remove an eyass, or nestling, goshawk from its nest. In the wild, mortality in young hawks is terribly high. By taking the smallest and youngest from the nest, not only is that eyass hawk's survival ensured, but survival of the remaining youngsters is greatly enhanced now that meals would not be divided among so many eyasses. There are many rules regarding the procedure. First, you have to obtain the landowner's permission. Second, there has to be more than one young bird in the nest. And third, the tree is then fitted with a metal sheath surrounding the trunk to secure it from any four-footed predators that might follow the human scent up to the young, flightless hawks.

The logistics of acquiring a young goshawk are even more complicated. You have to find someone with the ability and the equipment—such as metal spikes used by linemen and loggers—for climbing straight up trees. Then, all of the nestlings have to be banded, and the trunk sheathing materials have to be carted into the forest. All this is managed while dealing with a pair of enraged parent hawks. (Goshawks are large hawks that are terrifically aggressive—and vocal—when they consider their young to be in danger.)

We set about the project professionally. The climber we hired had been warned to wear both his thick leather motorcycle jacket *and* his helmet. He brought along his younger brother to carry the necessary gear. With a New Hampshire Fish and Game official directing, our climber climbed to the nest and soon lowered a bucket with three nestlings, which were quickly banded by the official. Jim was allowed to take the smallest of the nestlings to raise as a falconry bird. Meanwhile, the parents were "professional" as well in their defense of the nest! When the climber received an extra-hard *thump* on his head, he didn't realize a hawk had struck him.

Everything was done very carefully. The other two nestlings were placed back in their nest, the parents started to calm down, the climber descended with no further damage than a scratch on his helmet, the tree trunk was covered per regulations, and Jim went home with a young goshawk.

The fuzzy young goshawk became quite tame and oriented to us while living in his box in our bedroom, which is the whole point of taking goshawks as eyass birds. They are very high-strung creatures whose existence is based on instantaneous reactions. The females are quite nervous, but double that nervousness and you will have a better understanding of a tiercel (or male) goshawk.

It was fascinating to watch the little guy develop as dark feathers began to poke through his fluffy fuzz. But with the feathers growing out, the goshawk began to find his wings and to attempt scaling the wall of his box. It was at this point Jim had to leave on a weeklong business trip. "What will I do if he starts flying?" I asked him nervously. After all, this wasn't my bird.

"Oh, he won't be able to fly much," Jim replied. "Just spread out a tarp around the box in case he reaches the top to perch on the side."

Sure enough, the moment Jim left, the goshawk began fledging in earnest. I returned home from work that day to find Cadet triumphantly perched upon the rim of the box. To protect the wall-to-wall carpet from the random droppings inevitably left by a well-fed goshawk, I spread old bedspreads and tarps on the floor. When I came home the second day, he was perched on top of the portable TV on Jim's bureau. I used up our tarps and pulled out all my old beach towels to spread in strategic locations. On the third day, Cadet was on the top of the curtain rod, and there were one or two splashes of "hawkchalk" on the curtains. Out came the old sheets.

His flying practice was going great guns, and he had no problem using any spot in the room as a perching place. The bedstead, the windowsill, and my dressing table were all prime and desirable locations, it seemed. By the fifth day, everything in the room was draped in something, and I was out of anything more to spread. Added to all this, I could count on finding Cadet at least once a day stretched out for a snooze in the middle of my bed. I worried if I did not arise before dawn, I would wake to find I was sleeping with a goshawk. After five days of this, I was mightily sick of sharing quarters with a free-flying goshawk.

When Jim came back from his trip, I greeted him with the news. "Your bird can fly. He has been flying all around the bedroom all week. It is really messy and needs to be cleaned up. Time to move him outside to a mew!"

"Tomorrow I will put on his anklets and jesses. Then I will put him in the mew" was Jim's response.

"If that goshawk sleeps in the bedroom tonight," I said, my voice level, "you will find yourself sleeping alone with him." That very night Cadet got his anklets and his trip to his new quarters, and the bedroom was thoroughly cleaned of hawk droppings. It was wonderful to once again sleep in a goshawk-free bedroom.

CHAPTER 7

Injun on "Suffering Fools"

To use an old expression, Injun did not "suffer fools gladly." He could be the perfect gentleman when a small child came up to us, but sometimes when we were volunteering at crowded events, his gentlemanly behavior would be less predictable.

Injun was my assistant when I lectured on land stewardship and wildlife management in my volunteer assignments with the UNH Extension Service. Usually this meant meeting crowds face-to-face without being in a protected, roped-off area. I always tried to get a wall or a large display board at my back, but sometimes this was hard to do. Injun would be just fine until an adult with more curiosity than tact would step in behind us to reach out to stroke his back. A stranger touching Injun's back was tantamount in his mind to an attack. I was constantly on the lookout to prevent this from happening, but sometimes, despite my best efforts, the person would persist in reaching for my bird. If I did not get the opportunity to warn them off, Injun would do it for me. He would glare, crouch as though he were about to leap in an attack, and give his inimitable scream, getting the miscreant's attention very quickly.

Because he and I had visited so many schools, Injun had become quite used to children, enabling me to step into large groups of kids without his ever becoming upset. Children were instinctively much more considerate of Injun's "space" and this helped, too. But let Injun meet up with an adult he considered invasive or impolite, and he was not tolerant at all. Even worse, let an adult react with any derision, and an equal reaction was forthcoming from my bird. I have never been sure how he sensed this, but I saw the resulting actions on his part time and time again.

Injun's feelings on this subject were demonstrated clearly the day a photographer came to take pictures of our birds. The man had been out driving one day when Jim and I were walking, each with a raptor on our gloves. He was a news photographer for a paper in a neighboring city and asked to come take photos. We agreed and, on the appointed day, he took some lovely shots of the birds as we held them. Then he wanted action photos. I got Injun ready to fly in our backyard and tried to explain to the man how he could obtain the photos he wanted. He did not pay much attention to me. He had his own plans.

First, I lure-flew Injun, but the man kept stepping into the line of flight, so Injun had to keep replanning his flight trajectory. I could see my bird getting annoyed. From his perch in the tree, Injun would turn towards the photographer and flash in and out of being sharp set. It was a warning. The photographer was totally oblivious. Injun hesitated on the lure several times, and I knew it was because the photographer had moved again into the line of flight. I tried to explain, but was met with the challenge, "Well, is your bird going to fly or not?!" Finally I stepped under the tree in which Injun was sitting, and he dropped immediately to the lure now that the stranger was out of the way. The photographer got a superlative shot of Injun flying to the lure barely two feet off the ground. But, still, this man was not happy. The fellow was a very talented photographer, but he was unsatisfied and remained adamant that he *had to* get that one-in-a-million, flight-in-action shot.

He asked me to set it up so that Injun would fly across our backyard from a perch in a tree and to my gloved hand. So I cast Injun off my glove to the tree and walked to the desired location. The photographer moved in directly between us, his camera at the ready. I started to explain that Injun would drop from his perch to come gliding across the yard to me, but the photographer wouldn't listen. "Well, you know, if you will lie down on the ground under his flight path, you should be able to catch him in action as he passes you," I told him.

"No, I want the bird coming right at me," he responded, remaining upright in the middle of the flight path. I shook my head, returned to my station, raised my glove, and blew the whistle. Ask and ye shall receive.

"Jesus Christ!!!" the photographer shouted, now lying on his belly and as shaking and white as if he had seen a ghost. He had almost jettisoned his camera when he flung himself to the ground. Injun had dropped from the tree and started directly for me. With this fellow in his way, Injun had kept himself higher above ground than he normally flew when in a glide, at about five and a half feet. The photographer was probably five feet, ten inches tall. Instead of avoiding the photographer, as he easily could have done, Injun went directly for the camera. At the last second he bobbed up and over to clear the man's head before swooping to land on my hand. What this guy had seen in his viewfinder had taken the starch right out of his shorts. I knew that was exactly what Injun had intended to have happen!

"Uh, did you get the picture?" I inquired innocently.

"No!" came his short reply. The fellow hurriedly picked himself up and packed his gear. Clearly, photo ops had ended for the day.

CHAPTER 8

Moving to the Right Place

Flying Injun was getting to be so much fun, I hated to miss even one day. I was working full-time at an aviation company based at Manchester Airport ten minutes from home, so I was still able to get in our daily flights by coming home at lunchtime. One day, Injun almost became a menu item for someone else's lunch.

I would arrive home, hurry to find my hunting vest, tuck some chick pieces into a side pocket, grab my lure, and rush out to retrieve Injun from his mew. On weekdays the neighborhood parents were at work and the kids were all in school, so our street's cul-de-sac was a quiet, private spot to do our noontime flights. On this particular day and as I had every preceding day, I stood at the end of my drive to cast Injun off my glove. He flew to the rooftop of the house next door, as he had done so many times before. The moment he began his ascent, a wingtip brushed my cheekbone as a red-tailed hawk sailed over my shoulder. My first thought was, *How did Tabasco get out?* My next thought was mingled with sheer fright as I realized this was a wild red-tail in close pursuit of my Harris's hawk.

Blissfully unaware of his stalker, Injun landed on the roof and turned to face me. The red-tail seemed timid about landing on a man-made structure and veered off instead to land in a copse of trees in the neighbor's front yard a mere fifteen feet from my bird. This probably saved Injun from immediately being eaten by the larger and extremely predatory wild hawk. I pulled the lure from my game pocket and threw it down to the pavement at my feet. Like a rocket, Injun dove off the roof for it. As soon as he was on it, I grabbed one of his jesses and began running. Poor Injun! I had one jess in a vice grip, while he held the dragging lure with his free foot. He was literally doing splits and made it clear he was not happy about being carried upside down as though he was a child's stuffed toy.

I reached the corner of the backyard and thought, *This is silly. A wild red-tail is not going to chase after a human, even if the human is dragging what it expected to eat for lunch.* That's when our red-tail, Tabasco, hit the bars of his mew window with a resounding bang and let loose a blood-curdling territorial scream. I did not need to turn my head to look around. I knew the wild hawk was right behind us. I raced to Injun's mew as fast as I could. By the time I got him safely inside, the wild hawk had disappeared. My heart stopped its pounding, but I could still feel the tip of the wild hawk's wing brushing my cheek when I closed my eyes. It was likely the red-tail had been stalking us for days. By flying Injun daily at the same time and place, I may as well have set the table, inviting the wild hawk to dine.

From then on, I adopted what racing pigeon fanciers do and flew Injun at different times of the day. Fortunately my employer didn't mind if I took my lunch hour at ten, or one, or three o'clock in the afternoon. By constantly varying the flight time, Injun and I never had an uninvited lunch guest again.

Our subdivision neighbors in Londonderry had been very tolerant about the fact that we kept four raptors on our property, but the surrounding wooded areas were being developed into more subdivisions and light industry parks, so we decided to move to the country. Our criteria for the perfect place set the standard high. Finally we found what we wanted: a big, old house on twenty-eight acres with a huge garage, workshop, two barns, and a greenhouse in the tiny town of Deering, New Hampshire.

We had seen snapshots of the house and were attracted immediately by the beauty and history of the place. The house was built of brick in the late 1700s and had four massive chimneys. On our first visit, we saw something that had not shown up in the photographs. Every chimney was topped with a large statue of a phoenix bird with its wings spread. As we were admiring these statues, a big red-tailed hawk swooped low over our car and flew through the yard. Jim looked at me. "I think we came to the right place," he said. It was Fate. Any difficulty in having the house inspected, dealing with the tempestuous seller, or negotiating the sales agreement smoothed itself out like magic. Besides movers, we hired a flatbed tractor-trailer truck to transport our raptor mews the thirty-five miles into the countryside.

As soon as I could take a break from unpacking and settling in, I took Injun out for his first flight at our new home. He flew up to one of the tall chimneys and sat calmly beside one of the phoenix birds. My husband's words were true. We had come to the right place.

Jim and I continued our habit of hiking for miles with raptors on our gloves over the trails and logging roads of Deering. Once the locals found we did not mind them asking us questions about the birds as we walked the byways, we began to be well known. We were offered the use of neighbors' fields and timbered properties for flying. A local couple whose son-in-law was a falconer in Massachusetts gave us the run of their old, overgrown orchard, which turned out to be a woodcock cover. Injun and I never caught any of these very fast birds, but each chase after the elusive "timberdoodle," as they are called in New England, was an adventure in itself. And every adventure resulted in a stronger bond with my hawk.

Up the road a few feet from our house was an area known as the Overlook, which was a big field looking out over a huge vista of sky and the hills to the west. Injun and I made plenty of trips there for lure flying. Jim and I took a membership at a small game preserve, Chase Farm, only a few minutes away, mainly to work the pointing dogs we had at the time. At Chase, Injun became a seasoned hunter.

After several months of living in Deering, everybody knew that we were a bit different. We became used to hearing, "Oh, you are the *bird* people!" The UPS delivery man ceased asking what was inside those large, heavy boxes marked "Perishable." Instead, we would hear a cheery "Dinner's here!" as he dropped the boxes containing frozen quail off at the door.

CHAPTER 9

People in Kilts

A few months before the move, Jim and I were approached by Stephen Avery, the coordinator of the New Hampshire Highland Games, about bringing our birds that fall to present a falconry display at the annual Scottish Games held for two days at Loon Mountain every September. We had no idea when we signed up what a barrage to the senses this celebration would be. It attracted thousands of onlookers, hundreds of athletes and bagpiping competitors, multiple marching bands, sheep and herding dogs, and more people in kilts than I have ever seen in my life. Jim prepared a beautiful display mingling falconry gear with articles from his Scots heritage. Our exhibition area was tucked into the mountainside between the Historic Highland village and the staging for the Celtic rock bands playing in the beer tent.

Mr. Avery understood when we explained that the accommodations had to be such so that we could remove the birds from the hustle and bustle of the games. The sensory overload from the sounds, sights, and thousands of visitors turned out to be greater for the birds and for us than we had expected. For the birds, a quiet place to decompress in the evening proved mandatory. We were given access to an entire condo which provided the respite we needed for settling and feeding the birds, as they refused to eat amidst the commotion of the festival.

Added to these challenges was the Highland garb that we were encouraged to wear. Jim had inherited a full set of kilts from his family and looked very dashing wearing them. I opted for a more prosaic combination of khaki trousers, a white shirt, and a plaid scarf draped across my upper body and secured at my shoulder with a large decorative pin. Injun didn't seem to mind this or the tam on my head, which was something he had never seen before. Dealing with the huge throng of festival attendees while we were wearing unaccustomed clothing brought unanticipated challenges.

Once or twice a day, Jim and I would leave our helpers at our exhibit and walk about, each with a raptor on our glove. These walkabouts gave us a chance to stop by the many vendor booths. We posed for photo opportunities and told people where they could find our display. Each time, I scouted the long lines at the restrooms located in the main hall. On one trek, however, the line at the women's indoor restroom was quite short, so I jumped at the opportunity. Jim was carrying his prairie falcon, so he couldn't take Injun from my glove.

Few of the women coming and going took notice of the hawk I was carrying as I quickly made my way to an empty stall. Once Injun and I were inside the cramped area, I was faced with a predicament. I needed to slip my arm through the loop formed across my body by the plaid scarf, but there was no way to do this if I didn't find a perch for Injun first. The leash connecting my hawk to my glove was just long enough for him to make it to the top of the partition dividing my compartment from the neighboring stall. From this spot, he surveyed me with great interest.

I hurried about my business, praying that Injun would not move and would stay quiet. But Injun, the very soul of curiosity, turned around to peer down intently at the occupant in the neighboring stall. His bells clinked against the partition. In the space of a heartbeat, a human shriek split the air, and the door of the next stall slammed open. It took me a few seconds to restore my attire and fetch Injun down from his high perch. The woman's scream still echoed in the restroom as we exited the stall. At the sight of us, several women of various ages at the sinks doubled over in giggles. "Oh, dear," I said. "I owe someone an apology."

"You'll have to catch her first," one of the women managed to say between fits of laughter. "She was running when she left here!"

Flying Injun at the games was a surreal experience, so removed was it from the noise and activity I could see far below me once I climbed the ski slope. From the ground, the slope looked like a smooth, nearly vertical slant, but as one climbed, the footing leveled out to flat steppes, which would be perfect for flying Injun crisscross style high above the festival-goers. I could barely hear the announcement of our performance, but once I did, I stood and waved to the crowd. Injun and I blissfully completed his flights to the glove and to the lure. The flight demonstrations were the most relaxing parts of the two-day presentation. I nearly felt guilty for enjoying them so much.

CHAPTER 10

How High Should You Go?

We were invited by the Friends of Pillsbury State Park in Washington, New Hampshire, to do a falconry program that same fall. Jim was pleased to accept the invitation, as the park was familiar territory from his years at the nearby YMCA camp, and the area has always held a special place in his heart.

We got there early while the morning mist was rising off the lakes and ponds of the park. The place chosen for our presentation turned out to be the loveliest we have ever seen for a demonstration. It was a grassy point backed by a small lake bordered by low hills. The foliage was coming into peak fall color. The blue sky overhead and the colorful hills were reflected in the still water. Never have the birds had such a beautiful backdrop. Injun and I did a flight presentation showcasing his usual finesse. The setting, combined with the friendly park staff, the warm reception from our sponsors, and the appreciation of our audience, made this falconry demonstration our favorite of all the programs we had done.

A summer or two later on a morning in July, I got a call from the young woman who had been the intern at Pillsbury when we did the program. Our presentation must have made an impression upon her. Now she was working in the state office of the Division of Parks and Recreation. Her call was to ask an unusual question: Could we fly a bird on the top of Cannon Mountain? Aside from the experience of flying Injun at the Highland Games, I knew nothing about flying on a mountaintop, but I took a breath and answered in the affirmative. *Could a mountaintop be different from a ski slope?* I wondered to myself. The young woman said she would get back to us, and I thought, *Well, sure we can. There might be problems, but Injun should be ready by early September, and with plenty of time to work at it, he and I will be up for it.*

A day later, she called back with word that a commercial for an insurance company would be filmed on top of Cannon Mountain, and the casting agency in California would be in touch to coordinate being hired for the filming.

"When will this be happening?" I asked, thinking, like any logical soul, that film crews would seek a time in the fall when the color at the mountain was at its most spectacular.

"Next week. They plan to film on Thursday."

I nearly dropped the receiver. Injun had been put up for molt since early in March. Although he was just finishing his molt, he was still overweight, and I had not planned to start flying until cooler weather, perhaps in late August. I had eight days to get a very fat, out-of-condition Harris's hawk ready. "Sure," I answered with a squeak before I hung up the phone.

The first order of business, the *immediate* order of business I should say, was to get Injun flight ready. I usually do this over a period of two or three weeks. But I had only eight days. So Injun went on a diet, but food reduction alone will not do the trick. Sitting in his mew with a reduced food intake causes a hawk's metabolism to slow down, burning calories much more slowly. This state of slowed metabolism is called torpor. I had always found it helped Injun to lose weight and get into shape by walking. Not Injun walking, *me* walking. So every day I made extended hikes with Injun on my glove. His excitement at seeing new things, at shifting to balance against my motion or a breeze catching his feathers, and at occasionally bating off the glove if he got excited—all of these things worked to burn calories. I probably burned a few, too.

A call came from the California agency. The woman on the phone told me her agency was responsible for hiring and coordinating the film crew and actors for the commercial, and had themselves been hired by the advertising firm in New York City. The ad people wished for me to do a flight sequence, she said. Using a peregrine falcon would be nice, the advertising executives thought. I replied they were welcome to find another person for the job as I would not be flying a peregrine, but I could bring Lass, the peregrine I had very recently acquired. I volunteered Injun for the flight sequence. "That will be just fine," the agency lady said, and it was settled that Lass would be filmed for the close-ups while Injun performed the "stunt" of flying across a ledge on one of the highest points of the mountain.

I was to meet the crew on the appointed Thursday, at an early hour, at the Appalachian Mountain Club (AMC) building at the base of Cannon Mountain. I hung up with beads of sweat on my forehead. Flying a bird on a mountain ledge? How hard could it be? Certainly Lass, still molting and overweight, was not a candidate. Without being able to scout out hazardous conditions like resident red-tailed hawks or buffeting winds, flying on this mountaintop was sure to be a more difficult challenge than I had ever faced. Flying a peregrine (*peregrinate* means "to wander) under these conditions would have been even harder than flying a reliable hawk, so I would never have agreed to take it on without more preparations.

Injun and I continued our daily forced marches, followed by weighing him every day. Finally, on Wednesday afternoon he was approaching flying weight, so I turned him loose for one quick, successful flight. He still was heavy and relatively untried for the season. I would have to rely on his terrifically strong hunting drive and my skill at flying a hawk on a mountaintop (as yet, entirely unproven).

The next day saw Jim and me on the road as dawn was breaking. Lass, hooded and riding upon her cadge, which is a wooden box used to transport raptors, and Injun in his giant hood were in the car. We pulled into the parking lot of the AMC building right on time, but when we entered, there was no film crew to meet us. Instead, there was what looked like an assortment of sleepy college students reclined on every available resting place or chair, with nylon fabric backpacks and duffels strewn about. We glanced around and were suddenly greeted by a young man who spoke with a crisp British accent and who introduced himself as the director, while the rest of the "students" began to stir and pick up their bags (all filled with cameras and gear for filming as it turned out). We had mistaken the Californians for day-tripping hikers.

More arrivals came, and suddenly we were part of a crowd of ad agency account executives from Madison Avenue, executives from the Boston-based insurance company for which the commercial was being produced, the Californians, a pair of actors portraying the father and son of the commercial storyline, the director who had been flown over from London, England, and a grumpy-looking assistant director who, we were told, had assisted with the Morris the Cat cat-food ads. The acting agency person, who also could be mistaken for a student, turned up at my elbow to welcome us. It was one big party of nearly forty people requiring several trips on the Cannon Mountain tram to haul us all to the top of the mountain.

We found ourselves shuttled into the tram with the director and the acting agency woman. Just before our tram left, the manager of the state park came in to fix his steely glare upon us. "I don't want those birds anywhere near my tourists," he said.

"But our birds are perfectly . . ." was all I could get out before the director stepped between the manager and us. He murmured reassurances to the manager so smoothly and politely, the park manager was out of the tram before he knew it and we were on our way. Halfway up the mountain, I realized the manager thought we were professionals coming in with the Californians. He did not realize his bosses at Parks and Recreation had chosen us to do the filming. We, like the park manager, were New Englanders watching the Hollywood stuff unfolding around us. It was the first of many times during the day the director stepped in to handle matters, to level pathways and tempers. No wonder it was worth bringing the man over from London.

On the ride up, the director and the casting agency person filled us in on the scenario. "The script is called 'How High Should You Go?'" the director told us.

"But the crew is already calling it 'How High *Are* You?'" said the agent, rolling her eyes.

Ignoring her, the director quickly sketched out the storyline: A man and his son are hiking a mountain trail. They get to the top of the mountain, where the father sits down and starts to wonder if he has enough insurance.

We must have looked incredulous. "Excuse me, but where do a falcon and hawk enter into this?" I asked.

"Oh, a falcon flies over the father's head. And starts him thinking about insurance," was the answer.

Once we cleared the tram, Jim was left with Injun at the picnic area while I, with Lass, followed the crew out to a point where the view was the mountain across the Notch from Cannon. Except there was no view. The entire mountaintop was shrouded in thick fog. I was told to place Lass on a boulder while the director, assistant director, and cameraman set up for her close-ups. Filming would begin as soon as the fog lifted, the view appeared behind her, and the sun shone down. "What do we do until then?" I asked.

"We wait," was the answer. And we did.

For two hours we made small talk and looked at Lass, who sat and looked back at us. Suddenly the air stirred, the dense fog behind Lass rolled away to reveal the other mountaintops, and a beam of sunshine shone directly down on the peregrine. The crew filmed like mad for five minutes before the dense fog rolled right back in. All the time the crew had been filming, I had been able to assess the reasons *not* to fly on mountaintops.

One important reason had to do with the flock of crows that flew over as soon as visibility had cleared. They would certainly like to drive my bird off Cannon Mountain. The more important reason was that if one of my raptors should fly off, the next perching place was a long way away on the neighboring mountain. Should my bird choose to go there, which could easily be accomplished in one effortless glide, my route to retrieve him would be more than a hundred times as long because I would have to climb down the mountain (or ride the tram), cross the Notch, and climb the neighboring mountain (which did not have a tram). In the back of my mind was the uneasy thought that I had only flown Injun once after months of his being put up. What if I was misjudging how he would react? Flying on Cannon Mountain was too scary to contemplate. Inwardly, I shuddered.

When I left Jim at the picnic area, I was full of false bravado. He had looked around the area as soon as we were out of the tram and pulled me aside just as I had started out to follow the crew. "Nancy, you can't do this."

"Yes. Yes, I can do it," I had replied with confidence.

After nearly forty-five minutes more of watching the fog curtain, we felt the wind stir again. This time the fog cleared for good, and the crew got in twenty minutes of filming every nuance of Lass sitting on a rock before the assistant director said it was time to stop for lunch. Filming the flight sequence would begin on the chosen ledge right after lunch, he announced. I could hardly wait to get back to Jim and the picnic area. "Jim, I can't do this!" I said.

"Yes, you *can*," Jim now said firmly.

The catered lunch for the crew and the executives was marvelous, but I felt like a condemned prisoner eating her last meal. After lunch we put Lass into the giant hood for safekeeping, and Jim went out to assist me and Injun. The ledge was a narrow stage of rock at best ten feet wide and forty feet long which hung over a sheer drop. I was quaking inside as I prepared Injun for flight. The director began setting up the scene. "Where is the furniture?" he called out.

All morning long I had heard snatches of small talk in which "the furniture" was mentioned. "Here we are," the older actor called back. Suddenly I realized the term applied to the two actors who were playing roles in the commercial. The director put the father-playing "furniture" in the spot he wanted and then turned to me to explain how he wanted the flight to go. After his explanation, I looked around. There were about thirty people gathered at the sidelines.

"I want the set cleared," I said. This did not win me any popularity contests with the executives who had planned to watch the filming, but the director waved them off. The group went down the trail out of sight. "Can we do one practice run without the actor in the middle of the ledge?" I asked the director. Again, my wishes held sway. The director was allowing me the space to make decisions, he explained to the crew, because he knew he could not direct Injun. Only I could do that. *And it better be good*, I said to myself.

I put my internal butterflies aside and quickly planned out how we would fly Injun. Jim took a place at the far end of the ledge and held Injun while he waited for my whistle. I saw a boulder about four feet high at the opposite end of the ledge and scrambled up on it. I blew my whistle and raised my glove. Injun came like a shot. My confidence returned. After a long, boring morning, Injun was ready for action. I told the director the actor could now take his place and we could do as many takes as were needed.

With the businesspeople off the ledge, it was quiet. Besides Jim, me, and Injun, there was only the director, the assistant director, the cameraman, and the assistant cameraman, whose job it was to put lighted cans of Sterno underneath the lens to make it appear as though heat waves were coming off the ledge. Oh, yes, the furniture was there, too: a very handsome actor with carefully coiffed hair which had not moved a strand all day.

Jim took Injun and went back to his place. "Bend down," the grumpy assistant director said to Jim. "I can see you at the side." Contorting oneself is not easy while holding a hawk and standing poised over nothingness. "Step back another foot," the assistant director ordered.

"I can't," came Jim's reply. "My heels are hanging over the ledge as it is." I felt badly for Jim. He hates heights.

"Okay," said the director. I blew the whistle and Injun made a perfect flight right over the furniture's head.

The assistant director's face turned bright red. "I didn't say 'Action'!" he exclaimed in exasperation. Obviously he did not care for nonprofessionals like us making mistakes.

"That's all right," the director said kindly. "Will the bird do it again?"

Most times, Injun didn't like flying over strangers, and I knew he didn't like people in whom he detected impatience. The assistant director was making me tense, and I was not sure what my tension was communicating to Injun. "This time I am using the lure," I told Jim as I handed Injun off to him. I climbed to the top of the boulder again and had the lure at the ready. Everything was set to go.

"Action!" shouted the grumpy assistant director.

I blew my whistle and swung the lure. Injun came in a beeline across the ledge, dropping lower than before and nearly parting the hair of the furniture. It was the only time the man's hair moved all day. Injun sailed back up to hit the lure, then dropped with it into the shrubbery just below the far side of the boulder. I could see him following it all the way down to the base of the shrub, and I was afraid he would hurt an eye in the branches. I dove headfirst in after him, which caused the director to think I had fallen off the ledge until my husband assured him I was just going after my bird.

When Injun and I popped up from the brush, there were smiles all around. The director had already viewed the footage and had stopped it at his favorite spot to show me. There was Injun, filling the scene, his wings forming a stop-action teardrop about five inches above the head of the actor. The director was thrilled. We did not need to shoot again, which was good, he said, as the day was getting long and the son-playing furniture was growing a five o'clock shadow, so they needed to quickly finish filming.

We met the agency woman at the foot of the tram. She handed us a check for a thousand dollars. Injun and Lass had done a very good day's work, but the commercial, as far as I know, never aired on TV. We chalked the memorable day up to another unique experience we would not have had if it had not been for our birds.

CHAPTER 11

Thin Ice and Pheasants

Before moving to Deering, I had taken on the sponsorship of an apprentice, a young woman named Beth, who had her own red-tailed hawk. A requirement in New Hampshire is that apprentices hunt with their sponsors at least twenty hours each for two years. To ensure Beth would finish her apprenticeship neatly in the two-year period, I took her out hunting with me sometimes. This slender, comely young woman with no hunting background loved her bird so much, she had converted a bedroom in her condo into a mew. Beth was always up for learning anything new, so I invited her to a winter hunt at Chase Farm and told her to bring snowshoes. I knew we would need them in the deep snow of the fields.

Once at the farm, we left her bird in her car since we were flying Injun first. After I cast off Injun to take a perch in a tree, I walked ahead. Soon after entering the field, I thought I heard a sound behind me near where Beth was walking. I turned and asked if she had heard it. When she answered "No," I continued on. My hearing is poor, so I figured if Beth had not heard it, I must have imagined the sound.

Suddenly Injun was nowhere to be seen. I searched the trees bordering the field and could not sight him. We retraced our steps, looking for my bird, and I found where a chukar game bird had blasted out of a hummock. I could see the scattered ice and snow right behind Beth's snowshoe track. She had very nearly stepped upon where it was hiding. I realized then I had heard the chukar's bleating squawk as it took off. The sound was so alien to my apprentice, she had taken no notice of it at all. It looked like the chukar had headed straight for the alder bushes thickly clustered in the swamp between the hunting fields. That would likely be where Injun had gone. Beth and I might be less than expert at hunting, but he would have been in pursuit of the game bird immediately.

Beth started around the outside perimeter of the swamp while I headed straight in. In the black alders, it was impossible to move wearing snowshoes. I slipped them off to walk cautiously between the thickets. By now I was well into the swamp, and I knew when snow is deep the ice under it can be very treacherous because the snow acts as an insulator against the cold temperature of the air. I was treading with careful steps. Once past the thick part of the brush and now in the very center of the swamp, I saw my bird gorging himself on the chukar he had caught and killed. He let me attach my leash to his jesses and lift him and the remains of the chukar to my glove. So far, so good.

I took one step and the bottom suddenly dropped out from under my feet. I went through the ice and up to my shoulders in freezing water. As I fell, I cast Injun and his prize onto the snow. I managed to get my free arm up to crook my elbow over the ice. There I hung. I could not get a purchase on the ice with one arm to drag myself up, and if I sank down to the bottom, the mud would latch onto my boots with a suction-like grip. I was in serious trouble. It does not take long in cold water for a human's body temperature to drop, impairing muscle and brain function to the point the person cannot help herself escape. In a short time the situation deteriorates to become a matter of life or death. This dangerous predicament was much worse than my comparatively benign experience of falling into a snowmelt stream. People have died from falling into frigid water and being entrapped, as I now was. And, needless to say, it was *cold*.

I yelled for Beth, who answered me and gingerly came into the swamp—still with her snowshoes on—to find me. I wondered if an apprentice who weighed ninety-seven pounds soaking wet could pull me out. She may have been slight and pretty, but thank goodness she was wiry!

Beth grabbed my coat collar and heaved. She pulled and I struggled. Eventually we were able to get my upper body atop the ice. I warned Beth to step back so we both did not end up in the swamp water. I wiggled myself free until I could swing my feet up out of the water and onto the ice surface. By now I had practically no feeling in my fingers, so Beth assisted me in attaching my snowshoes. Every stitch I wore was soaked. My boots were full of cold water, and I was coated in mud to my waist. With absolutely no dignity, but with a great deal of gratitude towards my apprentice, I retrieved Injun and his game bird, by now mostly eaten, and made my way out of the swamp. Beth took my arm, pulling me along as we started from the field to my car on the hilltop above the swamp. It was becoming hard to move in my frozen clothes. My teeth were chattering during the drive home, the car's heater going full blast.

I would not soon forget the day, and neither would Injun. Aside from screaming and glaring at me after I launched him off my glove when I fell through the ice, Injun was very content with his day of hunting. He had pursued, caught, and killed his prey. Now his crop was full of his chukar dinner. For the hawk, it had been a highly satisfactory day.

Injun was not always so successful at Chase Farm. On another winter excursion, we chanced to flush a hen pheasant. Injun was out of his tree in pursuit immediately, but the hen went straight up for fifty or sixty feet and then leveled off to fly directly into the swamp. Injun was close behind. When he dropped down below the height of the brush, I lost sight of my bird. This time it was safe to walk across the swamp ice. There was barely an inch of fluffy new snow covering the surface. As I entered the alder thickets, I came across the fresh tracks of the pheasant. By this, I knew Injun had not been successful. Pheasants are very big game for a bird flying at only twenty-one ounces, but I had hoped the hens, smaller and without the spurs of the cocks, would be small enough for him to take.

I backtracked the trail of pheasant footprints and came to a long skid mark across the ice. It was clear something had slid across the swamp with great force. At the end of the skid mark, there were dual wing prints in the thin snow—the pheasant with a hawk on its back. I looked around, and there in a sapling sat Injun, dazed and shaking his head as though trying to clear his brain of fog.

The story written in the snow told me Injun had landed upon the pheasant, which in turn had dealt him a good solid kick. Injun's body had been the object propelled with force across the ice. He had managed to fly up into the small tree till he could gather his scattered wits, while the pheasant had hightailed it for thicker cover. Injun may not have been successful, but he learned a lesson about pheasants which he never forgot, and he *hated* to have game elude the grasp of his talons. Inside my bird a vendetta against pheasants was brewing.

How well Injun remembered his first outing on pheasants was demonstrated late the next fall. Jim and I had been at the upper field of Chase Farm to fly Tabasco, our old red-tail. We were walking back down, each with a hawk on our glove, when a cock pheasant suddenly flushed beside the path. Injun launched from my glove with such power that he pulled his jesses loose from my grasp and immediately gave chase. There was an exciting pursuit before the pheasant went into a hole in a stone wall. Injun peeled off to perch in a tree above the wall. As we walked over to see where the pheasant had gone, the big bird flushed again and the chase began anew.

I was a bit worried how Injun would handle this large cock and fretted when the two crashed through a hemlock limb hanging down over a small brook to disappear from sight. I ran to the spot and lifted the limb. There in the brook in several inches of water were both birds. Injun stood atop the cock's chest. He had pinioned the foot the cock had raised in an attempt to spur my bird. Injun's other talons grasped the head of the pheasant in a killing grip. Injun had figured out how to handle bigger, dangerous game. My hawk was not about to let himself be kicked again if he could help it!

CHAPTER 12

Hawkdogs

Although in the beginning our use of dogs bordered on accidental, our hunts became more exciting when we included them. The ability of a dog to scent and locate game is awe-inspiring. I had learned about other falconers using dogs for pointing and flushing, and I knew most of today's breeds of hunting dogs descended from those used in falconry. The subject fascinated me so much, I wrote a two-part series for *Dog World* magazine consisting of stories I collected from falconers actively working their raptors and their dogs together across the United States and Canada. I could hardly wait to try it myself, but one needs to have a well-trained dog accustomed to being around raptors in order to start.

Jim had been given a year-old German Wirehaired Pointer when the dog's owner relocated to the West. Mustache Pete was from a long line of falconry dogs (hawkdogs are what falconers fondly call them) and had been raised with birds of prey from the time he was born. Pete believed his mission in life was to protect our hawks and falcons. To his dying day, he was the guardian of our birds whenever we had them perched outside.

Pete was, as far as raptors were concerned, completely trustworthy. Injun, upon first seeing Pete, decided *his* mission in life was to warn all within earshot that there was a *damn dog* nearby by screaming at it!

Jim was eager to get dog and bird working together. I let him talk me into turning Injun loose while Pete quartered below. We would have been far more successful if we had thought to have game to catch on the ground, too. You can guess the outcome. Injun nailed Pete right on his big nose. The gentle soul lay down with bird still attached to his muzzle, as we raced to get to them. I had to pry Injun's talons out of poor Pete's nose. Pete's attitude, far from being defensive, was apologetic. The punctures to his muzzle were not serious but must have been painful. We took him home and fed him pizza as a reward for his bravery and his charity.

There was an interval of a couple of years while I raised my own German Wirehaired Pointer and started her on a training program. Her breeder shook his head over the proposal of using My Shadow (as I called her) as a falconry dog because her sire was known for his ferocity towards predators. At this task, our red-tailed hawk, Tabasco, showed his worth. As a dog-training raptor, he was invaluable.

Back when Jim had been an apprentice, we went out with Tabasco on his glove and me with Inga, who had been the leader on my now-retired sled team. One day when we flushed a rabbit, the dog, the rabbit, and the hawk joined into one tumbling mass as they went over a steep drop down the slope of a hill. Inga's journey ended with an *oof!* when her body crashed into a pine tree, while the hawk and rabbit continued tumbling until they parted at the foot of the slope, both somewhat dizzy and dazed. The rabbit got away; however, the partnership between Inga and Tabasco had been cemented.

When Pete came to our home, the partnership picked up seamlessly between the new dog and the hawk. But Tabasco was always in charge; that is forever the relationship between raptors and hawkdogs. Importantly Tabasco, not being a bird with a high metabolism and raging hunting drive like the Harris's hawk, could be counted on to give a dog a second chance. Our dogs were careful not to err a second time once Tabasco had pointed out their indiscretions.

When My Shadow had finished her training at obedience school, I decided to start working with the hawk. The first instance was to perch Tabasco on his two-foot-high perch in the backyard. I put Shadow on a sit-stay about ten feet away and walked fifteen paces. By the time I turned, her rear had magically been repositioned a mere six feet from Tabasco's perch. She sat, rear wagging, eyes sparkling, and body vibrating with expectation as she looked at me and then at the hawk.

I placed My Shadow back at the original ten feet from the bird and turned my back for the fifteen-pace walk to my station. I heard behind me a heavy thud, like a sledgehammer hitting the ground, and turned to see Shadow carefully relocating her hind end to sit at the ten-foot distance from where she had moved the moment my back was turned. The hawk was fluttering back to his perch. When Tabasco wanted to make a point, a two-foot jump down to land could sound like a boulder crashing to the ground as he thumped his emphatic proclamation. My hunting dog was all seriousness now. She practically saluted the red-tail. *Yes, sir*, her attitude conveyed. *Whatever you say, sir!* Tabasco had certified Shadow's graduation to hawkdog.

It was remarkable how thoroughly indoctrinated into the role of hawkdog My Shadow became from Tabasco's one instructive lesson. A week or so later, I had Shadow running loose in our yard. She started around to the backyard, but when she reached the rear corner of the house, she froze. She was still for a moment and then carefully backed up to stand in one spot. Pointers who are endowed with great genes and good training will "honor" another pointer already on point in the hunting field by becoming stock-still. My Shadow had seen Tabasco perched in the center of the backyard. By retracing her own footsteps and becoming a statue, she was *honoring* the hawk. I was amazed.

The next step was to get My Shadow bird dog experience and training, and for this we sent her off to a trainer. After moving to Deering
and signing up with Chase Farm, I could hardly wait to start Injun and
Shadow working together, but I knew if we had a repeat of the nose experience, it could harm the performance drive of my young, newly trained
pointer. This time we had done some research with other falconers who
used dogs and Harris's hawks, and we carefully adhered to what we had
been told: "Hold the bird on your fist and let the dog point a pheasant.
Go in and flush the bird, but do not release the hawk. Do it a second time.
This will drive your hawk nuts, but do not let him go until your pointer
has a point on the third bird. By now your Harris's will be expecting the
flush, so let him go as the game bird takes off. Your hawk will chase and
probably not be able to catch, as he has the disadvantage of coming from
your glove."

But, as foretold, the third time was the charm. Once Injun had seen
my dog put up three birds, he decided this "damn dog" was worth something after all. I could turn him loose to take a perch in a tree, from which
he had a much better chance for a successful chase, and he would watch
the dog. Once a point was established, the hawk recognized something
was about to flush, and he improved his perching location and became
ready to explode into a chase after the game bird.

The day came some years later when I had to get a new puppy. I
finally found another breeder of German Wirehaired Pointers and then
had to wait a month before we could claim the one we wanted from his
litter, but the breeder and his wife told all who came to see the pups, "This
one is going to work with hawks!"

As I drove her home in my pickup during Hurricane Floyd, she
climbed into my lap to sleep for the entire storm-tossed trip. "Nancy's
Storm Warning" had a few years before I began working her in the field,
however. This time I wanted to train my dog myself, and I had much to
learn first. There was an interval before the pup and I were ready to work

with raptors, but once I got Stormy trained, the dance began again. I had some expert advice in getting her ready this time. The expert told me to credit Stormy's genes, which suited her so perfectly for the role I needed her to fill.

"Storm-a-thon" has proven to be the smartest, most righteous hunting dog a person could be lucky enough to own. Having been raised with raptors, she was a hawkdog from the get-go. With her steadiness in the field, her remarkably talented nose, and an unstoppable work ethic, she has been a superb hunting companion for the hawk and for me. At the onset, of course, Injun let everyone within hearing distance know just what he thought of this new dog, but once he saw her produce game birds for him to catch, my Harris's settled into following the dog and watching for her to go on point.

Having a dog does not necessarily make hunting *simple* or *easy*. "Hunting" is a much more appropriate label for the activity than "finding" or "getting." With a high-drive-for-hunting hawk and a talented hunting dog, you have increased your chances for success exponentially, but there is always the opportunity for things to go wrong. When things are not going well, the hawk's yarak might be unloaded on the dog, so a falconer must always be on guard. Sometimes the aggression comes in the form of a strafing run over the rear of the dog, and sometimes it is a full-on grab of the muzzle. None of this means you have a vicious hawk, but indicates instead you have a hawk "on steroids" due to an overabundant drive to hunt and catch. Hawkdogs do not turn aggressive towards the raptor. The falconer needs to be close and spry to protect the dog if necessary, so it follows that the falconer needs to be alert and athletic to support both of her partners in the field.

Why would a dog continue to work with a hawk after it inflicted injury upon her? No matter the pain, the gain from being there is the big attraction, making each moment in the field, from a hunting dog's viewpoint, the best moment of all. An illustration is my beloved Stormy. She has worked under a number of hawks, and has given the same consistent effort with each. But there have been those days. On one occasion when the scent was not rising and she could not get a whiff of game bird, she turned to point the tree in which Injun sat. He immediately got sharp set, ready to teach that lazy dog a thing or two. I had to intervene quickly to prevent this from happening. At the end of Injun's hunting season, when I was unaware of an injury he had suffered that was making him cross, he pounced upon Storm's head. At this point Stormy was young, and I worried this might affect her drive to work alongside a raptor. Luckily it didn't.

Each year of working Storm in the falconry field has resulted in her becoming more proficient. I can rely on her to remain on point while a hawk that initially flew off in the wrong direction returns to take up a better position. Sometimes the adjustment in a hawk's location takes time as I walk off to retrieve my hawk. Stormy holds her point for as long as it takes—sometimes more than forty-five minutes—for me to return and move up to initiate the flush of the game bird. This means I have a very good pointer indeed.

My dog and I must find and flush game for my bird, for only then will we be judged good partners in his eyes and he will continue to work with us. My raptor views the chase ending with the take of game as the reason for life itself. For me, to watch the other two work together, to observe the dog's head swing about as her nose catches the scent and her body follows into a stone-still point, to see the mad pursuit or the hurtling stoop of my bird, and to retrieve my raptor safe and sound at the end are all I need to make the day perfect.

Not all days in the field, however, turn out to be perfect. Some seasons ago, with Stormy having passed her eleventh birthday, one of the worst things that can happen to a hunting dog happened, and this time it was not a hawk attack. Impalement upon sticks or other obstacles as they run through fields is a common cause of serious injury to dogs during a hunt. The previous winter southern New Hampshire had suffered a severe ice storm which brought entire trees crashing down. The Timberdoodle

Club, a place where we often went hunting for game birds, had been hard hit, and the clearing of the damage was ongoing.

In early fall I was in one of the Timberdoodle fields, hunting with Storm, one of my Harris's, my apprentice Abi, and Joe, an accomplished falconer. It was a golden, late-September day. Storm was hunting ahead of us, in and out of the covers on either side of the dirt road, when she jumped a big oak fallen during the winter's storm. I heard a yelp and saw her spin in the air in a somersault, tumble to the ground, and get up only to fall again. She rose to limp a few steps, and then was back to hunting. Storm is incredibly tough. Nothing stops her. I knew there was trouble, but had to call her back to me before I could do a damage assessment. What I saw when she returned to me made my knees weak.

Reluctant to be bidden away from hunting the covers, Stormy came trotting back on my call. Her left flank from the end of her ribcage to her point-of-hip and down her rear leg was laid open in a gaping tear. Her wound was a window to the visible dog. Stormy had connected with the thick, pointed spur of a broken branch on the downed tree. It had entered her flank to run down inside her leg, separating the muscle from the bone, as the vets told me later. She spun on the branch, and when she finished her somersault, it popped out her side through her flank.

We were in trouble. Abi whipped out her cell phone and called the Timberdoodle clubhouse. During the walk back, Stormy insisted on continuing to hunt. Nothing was going to deter her from her mission. I handed my glove, hawk leashed to it, to Joe and started dialing my Hillsboro vet's office on my phone, but his number was busy. Jim was on a return flight from a business trip. Mentally, I computed the plans for finding a vet, getting care for Stormy, picking Jim up, and getting a hawk home. My brain was whirling in a crazy spin of worry about Storm. Abi began calling her vet in nearby Peterborough.

Abi volunteered to go with me to the clinic, an offer I accepted grate-fully, as I was a nervous wreck after reevaluating Storm's injury. When we arrived, the vets were set up for triage. Storm was whisked into the operating room. Suddenly the door opened and the vet tech approached me. My heart skipped a beat. Was this woman coming to tell me Stormy's accident had become a tragedy?

"Is it all right if we snip off that bit of a skin flap on her eyelid while she is under anesthetic? She will never know, and she will be so much more beautiful without it," she asked me.

I mumbled my assent and took a relieved breath.

"See," Abi said, patting my knee gently, "she is getting cosmetic surgery!"

In due time a very drunk Storm-dog was brought out to me, complete with dozens of staples, a drain, and an Elizabethan collar, the plastic appliance used to prevent canines from licking or chewing at a wound. Abi and I were rescued when a UPS driver helped us load Storm's sixty pounds of dead weight into her crate. It was easier when I got home to just let Storm ride my shoulder as I lowered her to the ground. She teetered alongside me into the house, where I re-crated her (this was not easily done with the Elizabethan collar).

During her four-week recuperation period, Storm annihilated three Elizabethan collars. The backs of my knees became black and blue from where her cone of shame had collided with me. Her spirit— perky, bossy, and always up for adventure—never changed at all. During the following winter, I nearly lost her three times when the portion of her small intestine that had been poked by the limb shut down in a functional blockage. Each time, with vet care and much worrying on my part, she got better. Still, the horrendous wound and the ensuing sicknesses took a toll. The vets told me to expect arthritis would set into her leg, and that has happened. I do not want to strain her, but I need to work my younger pointer, Trouble. It is next to impossible to leave Storm at home when she knows we are loading the car for a hunting expedition.

On a trip out to hunt the fall after Storm's impalement, a falconer from Massachusetts joined our hunt, bringing his German shorthaired pointer pup and a young goshawk. I hunted with Storm and Smoky, one of my female Harris's, in the morning. We got the lovely action of several points and flight-chases but no success until, at the very spot Storm was injured the year before, she went into a dead-on, stock-still point, the tip of her tail aquiver. With the flush, my hawk sprang into a chase that ended in taking the chukar in good fashion. It was an exciting conclusion to the morning's hunt.

We lunched at the clubhouse and afterwards started back out to the field to work the other fellow's pointer and his goshawk. The falconer had watched Stormy all morning as she worked methodically. "Could we put the old dog back out?" he asked. His line of thinking, I am sure, was it would be better to work his green bird with a solid pointer, one that looked enough like his pup so his bird would not realize it was not his dog she was working over.

I had not planned to exert Storm so much, but she was delighted to be out for more hunting. She got a good point on a pheasant, but, when the game bird flushed, the excited goshawk dove straight for Storm and fastened to her head. The falconer ran to get his hawk off my dog. As soon as she was released, Storm was back to hunting. She got two additional solid points with flushes of big pheasants and his goshawk got two chases that afternoon, the goshawk having learned it was better to chase the game bird than grab the dog. By now the day was late. Stormy had to be tired, but she was energized from the hunt. She leapt into her place in the back of our SUV. By the time we arrived home, she had stiffened. I had to lift her down from the back of the car.

For the next week, I helped the old gal up and down the stairs. When I faced the onset of another hunting season, I wondered, *How will I manage to leave this dog behind when I am going out to do the thing she loves best in the world?* I am not the first hunter who has faced this dilemma, I know, in pondering how to tell a partner it is time for her to become "retired."

When things are going right between my dog and hawk, I think, *It does not get better than this.* During these moments I feel as though I have never lived so keenly as in this precious space of time. The teamwork between the hawk, the dog, and the falconer is for me the most thrilling experience falconry holds. For the falconer who is fortunate in having a good dog and a good hawk, it is nirvana.

CHAPTER 13

Bird Years

After moving to Deering, I was asked to provide a program for a big event held by the Cub Scouts. Programs done for youngsters are my favorites, and Injun's calmness with groups of children was a big asset. It was too bad, I thought, that the program had to be indoors and at night, as I would have loved to have flown Injun for them, but after arriving at the clubhouse, I began to envision a plan.

I had never flown Injun indoors before, but here I had a large rectangular room with windows with drapes that could be drawn closed (one of the biggest hazards in flying indoors is the raptor does not see clear glass as a barrier, and if the bird flew into a windowpane, it could easily break its neck). Behind me was a huge stone fireplace taking up nearly the whole wall of the rustic building. I sized up my audience: more than a hundred first-grade boys sitting amazingly still on the floor, all of whom, at the warning they could not see the hawk if they made noise, had become perfect angels. I told them about predators and birds of prey. I then made a bargain with my audience: If they would not move if the hawk happened to land near them, I would do something I had never done before. Could they keep the bargain? More than a hundred small heads nodded vigorously. I instructed the Scout leaders to draw the drapes.

"Okay," I said again, "I really mean this. You have to promise if the hawk lands beside you, you will not scream or run around." Again, I received the serious assent of the youngsters, each of whom, if the truth were told, would have been delighted if the hawk had landed next to him.

So began the debut indoor flight for Injun and me. I perched him atop his giant hood and walked across the room to turn and whistle him to my glove. He came as straight as an arrow. We tried it again, and he came again right to me. I went for a third flight. By now Injun was comfortable in the room. He flew over the boys' heads towards the adults sitting in chairs at the back of the room. There was some involuntary ducking from the grown-ups as he wheeled about and headed back to land on top of one of the andirons in the fireplace. He sat there teetering back and forth to maintain balance on his slippery perch. I knew when enough was enough, so called him to my glove.

The wonder of the program was not the accomplishment of indoor flight, but that one hundred six-year-old boys sat still for thirty minutes. They were an orderly, attentive audience, but at the end of the program one of the leaders confided in me, "You didn't make us adults promise not to scream and run around. We were ready to head for the exit for a moment there!"

Later, when I told Jim about the evening, I asked, "Were you worried about me, going to do a program alone at night?"

Jim laughed. "I never worry about you with that hawk on your glove. Anybody who tried to grab you would get his mind changed in a hurry. Injun won't let anyone get close to you."

When Jim and I present at schools, sometimes we touch on concepts of behavioral science older students will encounter in textbooks. Words like "imprinting," "instinct," and "involuntary reaction" are superbly illustrated by raptors. Sometimes we present to fifth or sixth grades because they have just read Jean Craighead George's classic, *My Side of the Mountain*, about a young man who goes to live on his own in the forest with a peregrine falcon for company. For younger children, our talks most often follow what I call "Predator 101," in which we explain how wild raptors live their lives and how they catch food to feed themselves and their young.

Whatever the topic of the day, we know we will have an attentive audience. The most memorable experiences from doing talks and programs invariably occur when we do demonstrations for children. Adults predictably ask the same questions, but one never knows what a child will ask. There are several instances from these experiences I shall never forget.

For instance, Jim and I once did a program for second-graders at Matthew Thornton Elementary in Londonderry. We kept the lecture simple and illustrated our words by having a hawk and a falcon there to show to the children. Part of our talk was based on explaining how our birds still had all their wild instincts, only they were not afraid of us.

Finally we told the children we would bring the hawk around so they could touch the bird. Our falconry school licensing enables this physical contact, as limited and protected as it is. I always choose our steadiest and calmest hawks for this, and I stress "touching" is not "petting," as raptors are not, nor ever should be, considered pets. I take the child's hand in mine and hold it to lightly stroke the breast of the raptor with a fingertip, the only part of the small hand that is exposed. The feathered breast of a raptor is very soft, not at all what is expected. Touch is one of the most basic of senses we have to learn about the world around us, so touching the hawk is an unforgettable learning experience.

On this particular occasion, the children were seated on benches forming a large square, with each student waiting for his or her turn as I walked around the inside of the square. As I started down one side, I saw a little boy down the row. He was waiting to touch the bird, but he wore thick winter gloves in a bright neon color. I knew the hawk was going to be startled by the vivid color, so when I reached the boy I told him he needed to remove his gloves if he wanted to touch the bird. He made me wonder if perhaps he was frightened of the hawk and thought the gloves would protect him. I hastened to assure him he did not have to touch the bird if he didn't want to, and the gloves were off in a flash. The touch was completed and I continued down the line of children, but when I heard him speaking, I stopped and turned.

The boy was turning his hands first palm up and then palm down to make a thorough inspection as he said to himself in the solemn tones of an elder statesman, "I suppose if it had been a *very* dirty bird, I should *have* to wash my hands." I realized this child must have been admonished by the adults in his life not to touch wild creatures, as they might be "dirty." I was glad the boy took the chance to touch, despite what he had been told. I have since wondered if he told his parents he had touched something "wild" that was not dirty at all.

There was another unforgettable occurrence with a little boy that happened at Underhill Elementary School in Hooksett. On this day I had the hawk for the flight demonstration and the peregrine falcon I brought with me to exhibit. It was a fun time, with a lively audience of first-, second-, and third-graders helping me watch the skies for wild raptors before I turned my hawk loose to fly.

At the end of my program, the kids lined up to return to their respective classes. I found myself beside the first-grade students, many of whom were itching to break out of line to come closer as they waited their turn to enter the school building. A pair of boys edged nearer. One of them was the most beautiful little boy I have ever seen. He was perfectly groomed, with neatly trimmed hair and shiny black oxford shoes. Dressed in linen Bermuda shorts, immaculate white kneesocks, and a starched white shirt, he was as crisp and well pressed as a haberdasher's model. He was accompanied by a tousle-haired friend wearing scruffy sneakers, worn dungarees, and a striped T-shirt.

The pair moved still nearer, bending the straightness of the line. The beautifully clad youngster's eyes were fixed upon the peregrine sitting on her perch, but he was hanging back behind his friend. The intrepid owner of the sneakers, meanwhile, was working hard to get my attention. I turned and smiled at them.

"He wants to ask you something," Mr. Scruffy Sneakers told me as the handsome child stood shyly behind him.

I turned to the shy boy and said, "Yes, what do you want to know?"

The child pointed to the peregrine and looked at me earnestly, "Is that a danger bird?" he asked.

An assistant teacher came over to shepherd the pair back to the line. She giggled, "Oh! He wants to know if the bird is dangerous!"

"No, I don't think so," I said, holding out my hand to stop her from herding the pair away. I turned to the youngster. "Are you asking me if this is an 'endangered species bird'?"

Eyes wide, he gave an affirmative nod to his head.

"Well, the peregrine used to be an endangered species, but now there are more of them. Now they are listed as 'threatened,' so the peregrine has made a good recovery and there are many living in the wild again."

Pleased with my answer, the little boy linked arms with his friend. The first-grade version of the "odd couple" returned to their places in line. I turned to the teachers' aide. "Do you have any idea how advanced a question that was for a first-grader?" I asked, shaking my head in amazement. I was flabbergasted to have had such a conversation with a six-year-old.

"Well, yes," she admitted. "We have been told he is a prodigy."

"Yes, I think so, too." I felt fortunate to have met this interesting duo of first-grade boys. I wonder if this child is elected president, will he promote environmental laws remembering when he, as a child, met a "danger bird" face to face? I wouldn't be surprised if his campaign manager is the school chum in the striped shirt and scruffy sneakers.

"Does he ever talk to you?" a little girl at Greenfield's elementary school asked me when Injun and I were there to do a presentation.

"Well, yes." I answered. "Not like a parrot talks in people language, but I know by how he holds his body if he is cold or unhappy or angry or interested. Harris's hawks are very 'talky' in Harris's hawk language. He has a nasty-sounding, loud scream if he is displeased about someone coming too close, or if he sees a strange dog. That scream says quite plainly, 'Get out!' He has a squawking, rasping call that sounds kind of like croaking or a creaking door that is his 'I am happy' song. Sometimes he has a very quiet, pleasant sort of a hum he makes when he is content and friendly. He is doing it right now as I speak to you. Can you hear him?"

She shook her head no. "Oh, this is hard," I said. "I never realized it before, but all the time I am speaking he is humming at me. As soon as I stop talking, he stops." I kept trying to stop my speech abruptly enough so she and the other children could hear my bird, but I could not manage it. Injun's "hum" was a low murmuring sound he made as I spoke . . . and the instant I was quiet, so was he. The children had to take my word for it, as they never got to hear his most companionable and friendly voice. I guess he reserved it for me alone.

Another school visit was equally unforgettable, but for hundreds of reasons which gave the day overtones of a horror movie. When I'm contracted to do a visit anywhere, I never guarantee to do a flight demonstration. I have to see for myself if the area is safe for flight. Until I have made a visual inspection of the area for hazards, I do not know if I will allow my hawk to fly. I especially need to see if there are any airborne dangers such as red-tailed hawks. Another concern is whether there are crows in the immediate vicinity. Crows will swiftly gang up to drive a hawk from their area. They are good at it, and many times I have seen "a murder of crows" (the term for crows in a flock or group) noisily driving away a wild raptor.

On this day, at an elementary school on the outskirts of Keene, New Hampshire, I had inspected the schoolyard upon my arrival. Everything looked fine. The playground behind the building was enclosed by surrounding trees and well away from hazards such as roadways and power lines. The first portion of the program would be a lecture I delivered to the student body inside the gym. Concluding the talk, I left the peregrine perched in the gym and walked alongside the principal as I carried Injun on my glove, onto the playground as the children settled around the perimeter. Just then, I chanced to look up. Two crows had taken flight from nearby perches and were flying off.

"Well, there goes trouble," I remarked to the principal.

"What do you mean?" he asked.

"That pair of crows looked like they were headed out on a mission. I hope they don't come back with some of their friends. If they do, it will be with the intention of driving my hawk away." I cast Injun off from my glove as the children watched. He took a perch at the top of a jungle gym, and I began to explain to the students how I called Injun in and how he would respond. Within five minutes I was shouting. It was impossible to speak loudly enough for the students to hear me. My voice was drowned out by the cawing of hundreds of crows. Every tree around the schoolyard had turned black with perching crows. Their cawing was a monstrously loud roar. It was a scene straight out of the Hitchcock movie *The Birds*.

I took a look around and made a guess that about six hundred crows, give or take a few, had joined my audience. Injun knew they were there for *him*. He flew down from the top of the monkey bars when I raised my glove. I cast him off again, and he wisely flew no higher than the height of the school equipment, choosing a landing spot on the crossbar of the swing set support. There was no doubt in his mind or mine: This "murder of crows" was bent on murder!

I raised my glove, but there was no need to whistle to him. Injun responded instantly. I caught up his jesses and turned to the principal. "I am so sorry," I said. "I cannot continue flying. It is too dangerous for my bird. Those crows are here to drive him away, and they mean to do it."

The principal was very understanding. "That is fine, Nancy," he responded. "I think the kids just got a great lesson about nature."

Please don't think Jim and I consider crows to be the enemy. Sometimes we enlist their help in finding raptors that have gone missing during a hunt or a flight. If a hawk has settled out of our view and for some reason is not returning on signal, or if a falcon has tired and has taken up a perch out of sight on the opposite side of the swamp, we need to know where to go to retrieve our bird. Telemetry can be a very fallible device in New England with its hills and heavy vegetation, but crows are almost never fallible. The first thing we do when trying to locate a raptor gone missing is to listen for crow vocalizations. When we hear their repeated, raucous calling, we follow the sound to see what or who has upset them. This has led us to successful retrievals on more than one occasion.

Meeting children, explaining raptors to them, and wondering what impact on their lives our presentations will have makes doing school programs very worthwhile. I still remember the live animal programs brought to my school long ago when I was in first and second grade.

My all-time favorite visits are when a kid stumps me, like the time I had concluded a talk to an assembly of second-graders. I always end with a question-and-answer period, a most important part of the presentation to young people. Often in primary grades, the first question sets the tone for every one of the next twenty questions, so I knew I was in trouble when the first question was "How old is the hawk?" It went just as I had thought, with questions on the bird's birth date, how old would he get to be before he died, and so on.

The hands waved wildly as each second-grader expressed his or her variation on practically the same question, but it was the final question that floored me. It was delivered by a little girl who fixed me with her stern seven-year-old eye and asked, "But how old is that in *bird years?*"

"Uh?" She had me neatly skewered with that one. I could not even manage to voice, "I don't know."

CHAPTER 14

The Importance of Being Injun

One day I lost Injun as he was pursuing a chukar into the swirling mist. Had he been unsuccessful, he would have returned to the treetops and begun working his way back to me, following the sound of my whistle. But the chukar must have gone to ground under one of the boulders at the woods' edge, taking Injun with him. None of us could find him and it was getting dark, with fog creeping up from the marsh below. We would have to leave before total darkness and come back the next day, hoping that Injun had survived the night, during which he might become prey for another, larger predator.

When we made the acquaintance of Randy and Colleen Martin, owners of a hunting preserve called the Timberdoodle Club in Temple, New Hampshire, the ensuing friendship resulted in our providing falconry demonstrations for members and guests of the club. In return, Randy offered us use of the grounds, which were abundant with pheasants and other game birds. Flying our raptors at Timberdoodle was wonderful as long as we were careful our own birds were not hunted by wild hawks drawn by the proliferation of prey. Injun provided many exciting moments for the spectators, such as the time he pursued a chukar right into a crowd of onlookers, scattering everyone across the field.

As exciting as that day was, it was the day Injun disappeared no one at Timberdoodle will ever forget. The day was a big event at the club, and a number of people came out to watch us hunt. Injun missed on a pursuit of a chukar. He knew where the bird had gone, so he took off into the dark evergreen woods to catch it . . . and vanished. It was one of those cool, fall days when the moisture floats as mist in the air. There are a number of large boulders in the area of woods bordering what Randy calls the Falconry Field. I knew chukars would go to ground beneath one to hide. A hawk, once it grabs game, is bound by the involuntary reaction of its talons grasping prey. I stood and listened hard, hoping to hear the tinkle of Injun's bells. Instead, I heard the mewing of the chukar, its death sound, so I knew somewhere Injun was nearby on his prey.

The air was so thick with humidity, it was difficult to discern the direction from which the sound had arisen. And then it was totally quiet. For an hour five of us searched to no avail. We put the dogs to searching but no scent rises in such weather, so the dogs were no better than we were at finding the pair of birds. In a case like this, knowing my bird and his loyalty to me was not going to help. Once Injun had grabbed the chukar, he was likely to be pulled down into the hole by his prey. He would settle down first to dine and then to let the effects of a huge meal pass. What would come later, when he finally emerged in an area full of aerial and four-footed predators, was what scared me. With the mist blowing around, there were no crows about to help us locate my bird.

It grew late in the afternoon, and darkness came quickly. It broke my heart to leave, but searching at dusk became totally useless. Sadly, Jim and I drove the forty-five minutes home with our dog and other birds. I was very aware of both the numbers and the types of predators frequenting Timberdoodle. There were hawks, owls, coyotes, foxes, and many other feathered and furred creatures who would love to feed on my Harris's hawk.

The next day we went to search again, but the dismal weather had settled in and gotten even worse. Nothing was moving in the field. Randy took his own hunting dogs and searched for miles, thinking perhaps Injun had flown out of the field. Jim made gloomy prognostications about the unlikelihood of Injun surviving a stay at Timberdoodle.

On the third day Jim had to return to his office in Boston. "Are you going over to Timberdoodle?" he asked as he left for work.

"Of course," I replied. My hopes were dim, as it was now actively raining. But as I drove over towards Temple, the weather began to clear. A front was blowing in, and it was sweeping the gray clouds out ahead of it. By the time I drove through the gates of the Falconry Field, the sky was blue with huge, puffy white clouds and the sun was shining brightly. As I got out of the car, I heard the sound of bells high in the trees at the other side of the field. I grabbed my lure, swung it high, and immediately a dark shape darted down to seize it.

I quickly knelt down and caught up Injun's jesses to secure him to the clip on my hunting leash, but I would have had no difficulty convincing him to come home with me even if I had not attached his jesses. He looked like he had gone through a wash-and-dry spin cycle. And he was ready to go home. I picked him up on my glove, but before I could open the car door, he was on the window glass, clawing at it to get to his giant hood and giving me a look that said, *You have* no idea *what I have been through, and where on Earth* were *you when I was ready to come home?!*

From the windswept, sunny field I called Jim at his Boston office to tell him the glad news. As I drove out, I stopped at the clubhouse and rejoicing began there, too. Injun was such a personality, it was hard for anyone to accept he had been lost. Now he was safely back and things could return to normal.

Fall became our busiest season. Free weekends for hunting were harder to schedule as we accepted more demonstration and exhibition engagements. One of my favorites was an event called Ducker's Day. The setting was an old farm near Durham. The day was a celebration of all that Great Bay, a large estuary, has meant to the region from the history of the gundalows (flat-bottomed cargo vessels) plying the bay to carry goods and supplies, to the duck hunters of olden times, to today's fishing industry. Celebrated, too, were the conservation of wildlife and the environment of the inland estuary. At Ducker's Day, set in a field behind the farm buildings and along the shore of Great Bay, there was great food, music, decoy carving, retriever demonstrations, tours of the re-created early nineteenth-century gundalow, and more. We set up a falconry display and did our flight demonstrations in the fields away from the exhibits.

My favorite part of the day was visiting the artisans' tent to see the paintings and wood carvings on display. On one occasion, I grabbed a moment to visit a friend who was a very talented wood-carver. Jim White's display included many types of beautifully carved birds. I had Injun on my glove as Jim and I talked. Suddenly I realized Injun was getting sharp set and looked about ready to make a lunge at Jim's wooden songbirds. This caused some merriment among the other artists. Jim's work was so lifelike that it had gotten a reaction from my bird. Soon I was being hailed by another carver, "Bring him down to see my birds! Oh, please, bring him down to see mine!"

I glanced down the long row of tables, and my eye was caught by the second carver's work. It was awful. This carver's birds looked exactly like the wooden sticks from which they were made. The angles were all wrong for the heads, wings, and legs. The carver, well intended as he might have been, would have been better advised to take up another craft. I was trapped! I quickly declined his invitation with the excuse that it was almost time for my flight demo so I should be getting over to the field. The carver plaintively begged me to bring my bird down to see *his* birds. There was nothing for me to do but to stroll down to his display.

I didn't want the fellow to be disappointed when Injun failed to show any interest. So when we reached the man's display, I turned ready to hasten away. The man sighed with pride behind his bright red cardinals, yellow finches, and all sorts of other highly colored but badly carved birds. Injun immediately got sharp set again. His eyes were riveted on the cardinal, but he would have been happy to jump on any one of the man's carvings. The carver was thrilled. His carving was so good, even the hawk was fooled, I heard him telling everyone. I escaped and headed out for the field. "Injun, you have no taste at all," I muttered as soon as I was out of earshot.

Injun surprised me in other ways, as he did once in front of a room full of adults and children at the Amoskeag Fishways Learning and Visitors Center. This museum highlights the history of the Merrimack River as an ancient fishing place. The center owes its existence to a partnership between the Public Service Company of New Hampshire, the New Hampshire Fish and Game Department, the Audubon Society of New Hampshire, and the United States Fish and Wildlife Service. It holds many conservation and wildlife programs for the public. This is what brought Injun and me there one evening.

The small presentation room was filled to capacity. Two-thirds of the room was taken up by seating, and the front third I shared with a huge ninety-gallon fish tank filled with a school of medium-size fish. The entire school swam together in quick darting movements, making turns in unison at each end of the tank. It was typical evasive prey movement, and it was driving Injun crazy. I was trying to give the presentation, and he was doing his best to leap off my glove to get to the aquarium. There was no way to distract him. Finally I asked the woman in charge to cover the aquarium with a sheet. That accomplished, Injun was able to settle down on my glove.

I am sure the audience found this episode educational. So did I. As well as I knew this bird, it was a good lesson in how much at the mercy of his hunting instinct he was. It had never occurred to me that Injun would be so enraptured with the fish, but, whether a school of fish or a covey of quail, the movements of prey animals were all the same to him.

During the eleven years Injun and I were flying together, he and I were partners, although I was quick to explain, "I am actually the *junior* partner, as Injun is the better hunter of the two of us." This always brought chuckles from onlookers, but the fact was we were uncannily attuned to one another. As readily as he took cues from me, I was reading my bird every moment. I could scope out an area and know immediately if it would lend itself to flying with Injun, as I knew exactly where he would end up taking perches and what his trajectory would be on a path back to me. And, by now, I had to say he was extremely *cooperative*, as much as I detested this overused reference to Harris's hawks. He enjoyed every outing, as for him each one constituted something of a hunting event. He even launched into a full chase on a smaller bird at an Audubon sanctuary, which delighted (thank goodness!) the audience of bird lovers.

The connection between Injun and me was so strong that I was able to pull him off the chase of a game bird gone to cover by enticing him to a different location where I knew another game bird could be flushed. Whenever I flew him, I could close my eyes after his release, point to a spot, and know he would be there waiting for me when I opened my eyes. The two of us were working as if one mind was directing us.

After a strenuous flight demonstration, I would sit on the ground with Injun perched on my knee. Suddenly a tug would come at my necklace or I'd feel nibbles on the clips of my vest. I might be giving a presentation when my whistle would suddenly fly by the end of my nose as Injun tossed it playfully from around my neck. I always knew, however, that my partnership with Injun enveloped me and changed me far more than it changed my hawk.

At the Overlook to lure-fly one day, Injun was in remarkably fine fettle. He had reached a superb level of conditioning, and as I managed to elude him with the lure, he turned to come back for re-passing. He was about ten feet above the ground, the dark of his back showing as he circled me with one wing pointed down and the other pointed skyward. When he turned his head to gaze at me, I freeze-framed the image in my mind and said a prayer: *Please, Lord, if someday I'm unable to speak or to communicate with the world, let me relive this moment over and over.*

For all of the profound feelings I had, there was no sugary sweetness in this relationship, and certainly none in this raptor. I cannot say Injun loved me. Terms of endearment are never appropriate when speaking of a hawk or falcon. I loved Injun, but it was not the same feeling that I might have towards a pet that courted my affection and depended upon me for care. Injun was too independent for that. I love my husband; I love my children. But, do I love my heartbeat? Do I love my right hand? This is what Injun was to me. As much as I might feel he was a part of me, Injun was "the boss," the "senior partner." As difficult as it sometimes was to satisfy this finely tuned taskmaster, whenever he flew, my heart flew with him.

PART TWO

A TALE OF TWO
PEREGRINES

CHAPTER 15

Tapped for a New Role

The peregrine was beautiful. His dark eyes held mine in a hard, unblinking stare. A furious hiss from his opened beak was barely audible. As I withdrew my left hand, now ungloved to move a leash about, a talon flashed by, piercing the fleshy part of my palm. The legendary reputation of the peregrine falcon as the fastest creature on Earth was no far-fetched fantasy, but as real as my blood welling from the puncture. Its fame as the fastest living creature comes from the peregrine's hunting method, a dive called the stoop, in which the falcon drops from on high at speeds of over two hundred miles an hour. But this bird, sitting perched and in recuperation from an injury, had lashed out a taloned foot like a strike of lightning. In the air, or earthbound, peregrines are deserving of their reputation for speed.

The falcon had arrived earlier that day from Squam Lakes Natural Science Center, an educational facility and wildlife rehabilitation clinic in Holderness, New Hampshire. His arrival had required weeks of planning, set in motion by a telephone call from Dave Erler, a rehabilitation specialist at the center, saying that one of our state's native-born peregrine falcons had been found two weeks before and was brought to the center for treatment for what looked initially like a broken wing. A veterinarian later determined the wing was dislocated. Now, having had surgery and treatment, the peregrine was healing. At this point, if the wing would ever be strong enough for release was anyone's guess. Dave hoped that the falcon could be returned to normal flight and released back into the wild.

"I have been talking with the Concord-based federal biologist, Michael Amaral," Dave explained, "and we feel that you and Jim are the only people in the state qualified to work with this bird. It needs falconry techniques to get it strong enough for release. If the wing proves to be so damaged as to prevent the peregrine from being able to resume normal hunting, then, of course, the science center would like it to stay here as an educational bird. But Michael and I agree, if at all possible, we want this bird rehabilitated and released to the wild within New Hampshire."

The question was whether we were willing to take on the difficult work of training the falcon, a task that takes hours out of every day. I knew the answer before it passed my lips. I suspect Dave was also fairly certain of what it would be.

Jim and I had attained the senior rank of master falconers and had developed reputations as advocates for conservation and wildlife management. Some of our presentations on raptors and falconry had been done at Dave's own facility. Dave knew we were keenly concerned with the population of wild falcons in our state.

Falcons are marvelous creatures. They have physical characteristics enabling them to complete prodigious feats of aerodynamic skill, but the falcon psyche is a fragile and complex mix of utter stupidity, seemingly mystical sensory capabilities, and a swiftness of instinct that leaps ahead while humans are still pondering the moment. Handling a falcon, therefore, is not unlike unlocking the answer to the infamous puzzle box in

Dan Brown's thriller, *The Da Vinci Code*. One false move, and the puzzle box is ruined and one will never be able to get it to give up its message. Falcons are like that. It takes knowledge and skill in order to be successful handling one. Go off in the wrong direction, and the falconer cannot back up to make a correction. One is left with what, in the historic language of falconry, is known as a "mar-hawk," a falcon so ruined it will never work in partnership with a human, and it will be a most unpleasant, even dangerous, companion every time a person must interact with it.

My husband's experience with falcons had begun years before with a prairie falcon named Tater. Tater was a gift to Jim from a much older falconer named Tex, a man who had learned falconry as a youngster from some of America's renowned masters of the craft. Tater had been purchased from a breeder as a young bird by another falconer who had recently attained the rank of general (the next level above apprentice) and so was allowed by law to buy the bird. Prairie falcons are notorious for being high-strung and for requiring especially skillful handling. In his inexperience, the falconer made mistakes, and the young falcon soon became the worst of mar-hawks.

The man turned to Tex, whose skill and patience saved the bird. Indeed, Tater's first owner told the story of going to visit them and finding Tex stretched out snoring in front of his television set with Tater on his chest asleep, her head tucked beneath her wing. The young falcon and Tex were like an old married couple, and, in captive-bred falcons purposely imprinted on humans, this is exactly how the relationship appears. On her maiden flight over a Maine potato farm, Tater landed and caught herself a good-size tuber protruding from the earth, thereby earning her unusual name.

A few months later, Tex had to leave the Northeast to follow his job. There was no living arrangement for keeping Tater in his new location. Tex and Tater's first owner talked over what to do and decided that because my husband was instrumental in legalizing falconry in New Hampshire and was well known by falconers throughout New England, they would offer Tater to him. To save them a long trip, a meeting was set in Concord, New Hampshire, at the home of Steve Wheeler, a biologist and the falconry coordinator with the Fish and Game Department.

This would be the first time we met Tex. A generation ahead of us in age, short of stature, round-faced and jovial, he was not what we had expected. With his twinkling eyes, cheeks covered in white stubble, and stocky build, he looked like Santa Claus.

Shortly after the Mainers arrived, we headed out to a nearby field to watch a flying demonstration with Tater. At the same time, Tex told Jim everything he could about the basics of handling the prairie falcon. Tex also gave Jim the cadge Tater rode upon whenever they traveled in a car. A cadge is a wooden box, open on the top and padded on two sides for perching. The traditional method of transporting a falcon is to have it perched and tethered to a cadge and hooded so it does not become frightened. There it rides as regally and calmly as if it were perched at home.

Tex gave Jim a hood he had made for Tater and a handmade lure as well. His open-handed munificence was as appreciated as it was unexpected. To Jim, it seemed just like Christmas Day. Many years later, Jim still has Tater's homemade hood in a place of honor among the fancy, exotic, and antique hoods that make up his collection. Jim's falcons ride upon the sturdy cadge built by Tex. Tex's lure, which looks like a squashed football, works better than any other lure I have ever used. Jim teases me because I borrow it incessantly.

While Tex was with us, he regaled us with stories of the great falconers who had taught him and of all the falcons he had known. We could have listened to him for hours, but it was getting dark and the wind-driven snow was pelting down hard. Before the Mainers left, Tex told us a final story.

When he was young, he had followed several falconers around as if they were gods from Olympus. Tolerating his presence underfoot and answering his many questions, they eventually let him help with the care of their falcons. The day came when they handed Tex a glove, pointed to a raptor, and told him to "go get your falcon."

As he stood in the doorway with the snowflakes swirling about him, he said to Jim, "And now it is time for *you* to go get *your* falcon." Then he stepped out and closed the door behind him. We stood there stunned. The scene was like something out of *The Night Before Christmas* (except for the part where Santa disappears up the chimney).

Tater took readily to Jim's careful handling and proved to be a loyal, able falcon he flew regularly. As she had with Tex, Tater had a love affair with her new master. I became resigned to sharing my husband's heart with another female. In fact, I told him he could have as many mistresses as he chose, but every one of those "other women" had best be growing feathers!

As for this injured peregrine, we were happy to accept Dave's proposal. Like Dave, we believed the rehabilitation of raptors is benefited by the use of falconry knowledge. Falconry licensing and rehabilitator licensing have very specialized and different requirements, however. It was mandatory for the regional US Fish and Wildlife Service permits office at Hadley, Massachusetts, to agree to the bird being under our care and to our training and flying it. For us to have a wild peregrine falcon without proper authorization would be highly illegal under federal and state laws.

The phone call concluded with my unqualified "yes," even though Jim and I knew that the dislocation of the peregrine's wing could be more catastrophic than a break, as soft tissue healing can take much longer than bones take to knit. My heart was pounding with excitement in the anticipation of working with a wild falcon as I hung up.

There is literally no way to condition or to test a formerly injured peregrine for flight readiness without actually flying the bird. When in hunting mode, a peregrine falcon will fly high above its airborne prey. Once the prey is spotted, the peregrine folds its wings to drop swiftly down and deliver a strike with its feet and talons. Hawks, in contrast, take a perch to watch for their prey to venture into the open. Then they swoop down with their wings extended in a glide. This means they can be effectively conditioned in a large enclosure known as a flight cage. Flight conditioning of injured peregrines is altogether different. Nothing quite compares to the force the wings of a peregrine falcon must withstand while in a dive. We knew that the fitness level required by the dive could be beyond the capability of a bird so injured it could be picked up at roadside. The successful rehabilitation of this peregrine back to the wild would not be a sure thing.

To train a wild peregrine that had learned to survive and make its own way was an experience without precedent for us. I immediately began thinking in terms of time schedules and dates. Suddenly it hit me that I had contracted with a breeder out west to purchase a four-week-old female peregrine. By the breeder's reckoning, my eyass peregrine would arrive at the end of May. Jim had a hawk and two falcons of his own, our living to earn, and a horrendous commute as well, so I would be responsible for training two peregrines at the same time—the wild adult male and a young captive-bred female. I mulled over the idea. As busy as he was, I knew I could rely on Jim for experience, advice, and assistance. That, at least, was one plus in my corner. Of all the fifty-odd springs of my life, I mused, this one would be remembered as the "peregrine spring."

Finally, I called Michael Amaral, whom Dave had mentioned in speaking about rehabilitation of the falcon. Michael told me it was a two-year-old tiercel, or male, hatched from Holt Ledge in Hanover. He thought we could be signed onto Squam Lakes Center's existing rehabilitator permit as subpermittee rehabilitators. I was not as certain. The permits office has never been casual about a possible mixing of falconry and rehabilitation licenses.

Training the falcon would necessitate it coming to our location. Michael and Dave were in agreement. Both understood enough about falconry technique to know it is based on trust and positive association. Michael felt a solid endorsement of us from the Fish and Game Department might carry weight with USFWS. "I banded this bird myself in 1999, and I want to see it go back to the wild here," Amaral concluded. Optimistically, we made tentative plans about how and when to transport the peregrine.

A few days later I received an e-mail from Michael. The USFWS permits officer required us to obtain our own wildlife rehabilitation license, which involved a time-consuming and laborious process. Absolutely, he said, the peregrine would not be allowed to come to our location without that permit. I called Michael to share my gloomy prognostications on how long it would take.

"I guess there is no way to get it all done in time to help this peregrine now, Nancy, but I would like for you and Jim to obtain your permits. Just in the event of this happening again, we can keep a bird from having to be sent out of state," Michael said before he asked me which facility in the Northeast I thought would be appropriate to rehabilitate the peregrine. I gave him my best advice with a heavy heart, unwilling to accept we would not have the opportunity to work with the falcon. "I did get a wonderful letter of recommendation about you and Jim from Steve Wheeler at Fish and Game," Michael said. "I am going to forward it on to the permit office anyway." There was nothing left for either of us to say. Our mutual disappointment had colored the conversation. Michael really cared about this falcon he had banded as a fuzzy youngster.

The next morning I made a call to the permits office about becoming licensed "rehabbers." The man in charge of migratory bird permits had taken the day off, so I told the woman who answered his phone that I understood a permit would come too late to help this particular falcon. To my surprise, she suggested ways to speed up the process, and my disappointment began to fade.

I left a message for Michael saying that I would complete everything quickly enough so that I could rehab the injured falcon. Michael was also buoyed by the woman's assistance. "We are going to get the transfer of this bird arranged, or I will have to have a very good reason why it cannot be done," Michael told me.

I downloaded the regulations regarding rehabilitator licensing from the USFWS website. An entire page listed the documents that were required, including a description of our rehabilitation experience and training and the birds we had worked with, along with a letter from a rehabilitator who could vouch for our experience. A report of our raptor facilities was required, along with appropriate diagrams, photographs, dimensions, and even a description of the flooring. A letter from a rehabilitation facility willing to lend use of their flight cage was needed. Also necessary was a list of what we would feed the "rehabilitees" and an affidavit from a federally licensed rehabilitator, again, reflecting knowledge of our training and qualifications, and promising assistance should we require it. The fourth item on the list was a letter from our local Fish and Game conservation officer indicating a need for rehabilitation skills in our region. Another requirement was a signed statement from a licensed veterinarian agreeing to provide medical treatment.

We would have to apply for, be approved, and be permitted under the state as wildlife rehabilitators. A copy of the license (which is not valid unless one also holds a federal permit) had to be enclosed with the application. We needed a letter from a public educational or scientific institution (including federal permit numbers) stating willingness to accept either the carcasses of birds that died while in our care or live birds deemed non-releasable. I set to work immediately to satisfy all the requirements, relying on the federal clerk's suggestions such as combining requests for requirements to fulfill to agencies that could satisfy several at once.

After contacting the permits officer, Michael called me again. "He restated you have to go through the entire licensing process, Nancy, but he did promise when your application came to his desk, he would process it right away." This was a huge concession for the Migratory Bird Permit Office to make, as we had been told there was a months-long backlog of paperwork. We were approaching a formidable government office for licensing, the same office staff that held our lives in their hands whenever it came time to renew our falconry licenses.

Despite the promise made to Michael Amaral, we knew there were no "shortcuts" and that if every *t* was not crossed, every *i* was not dotted, the wildlife rehabilitator license would not be granted and the injured peregrine would not be coming here. I was in a state of nervous excitement over the idea of working with the peregrine. Fulfilling all the criteria required to obtain my rehab license had become an obsession. This falcon filled my mind every waking moment, and at night I dreamed about the peregrine.

CHAPTER 16

Suspicious Characters

The realization that government and conservation agencies would entrust a wild peregrine into our care and make efforts to speed our qualification process brought my mind back to when Jim was trying to push forward legislation for falconry. Obviously the perception about us had changed since then, but the memory of being regarded as "suspicious characters" was still fresh. I think every citizen, aware they are being watched by a federal agency, feels some form of dread despite being guilty of absolutely nothing.

When Jim had first contacted the North American Falconers Association about entering a falconry bill, officials of the organization told him we would be investigated by government agents and would receive phone calls from paid government snitches with enticements to commit unlawful acts such as trapping and selling birds of prey from the wild. The calls and overtures from agents would be part of a "sting" operation to entrap us. We thought the association officials were exaggerating. They weren't.

As soon as Jim entered his bill, we realized we were being monitored. A covert sting conducted by the US Fish and Wildlife Service called "Operation Falcon" had occurred not long before. Although this operation was touted as a success in the immediate press releases from the government agencies, it ended with only a handful of convictions for a few relatively minor charges. Simply, there was no black market trade in raptors such as had been put forth, and questionable tactics were used to attack falconers who had never broken any laws at all. During the process, falconry birds were confiscated from their legitimate owners, never to be redeemed.

These actual results of Operation Falcon were not broadcast, but we became conscious that an arm of the government might be eager for a big score. We had no idea which agency that could be, but we were the most available "perpetrators" on which to pounce for no other reason than Jim's lobbying to make falconry a legal hunting activity. The phone calls we frequently received proved the warnings from NAFA.

Sometimes the caller would offer to "help" with Jim's efforts to legalize falconry. Always the topic would evolve into a request "to get me one of those *para-grines.*" The implication was that a peregrine could be gotten outside the law. Ridiculously the same individual did most of the calling, although he took on various personas (and some ludicrously bad accents) to disguise his voice. I grew up in the South, so a sorry attempt at adopting a southern drawl is something I recognize.

"Mister, I don't smoke and I don't chew, and I don't go with boys who do!" I finally snapped into the receiver one day after enduring a round of these attempts to lure us to break wildlife laws.

"Huh?" the caller was startled into saying.

"That means," I explained emphatically, "neither my husband nor I do, or plan to do, anything unlawful. And neither of us wants to have anything to do with anyone suggesting unlawful behavior. I am really tired of your stupid calls and your stupid accents, so why don't you give it a rest!" I slammed the phone down.

Next we started getting house calls. Jim had extended an invitation to a man who said he and his sixteen-year-old son were very interested in birds of prey. They were anxious, the man said, to meet Jim to learn about falconry in the state (which did not yet exist) and to become falconers themselves. We were in for a surprise when they arrived at our doorstep. The "father" was well-groomed and was wearing a suit and topcoat. The "son," who looked more like twenty-six than sixteen, also wore a suit and a topcoat. Jim invited them in to talk about falconry, its legislation in New Hampshire, and his plans to become licensed and obtain his first hawk. Jim's mew was not yet completed. The pair expressed curiosity about the building, so Jim took their home phone number and promised to invite them to see the finished structure.

Once the mew was completed, Jim handed me the paper with the number and asked if I would call the father and son to let them know they were welcome to come see it. Oddly, when I dialed the number, it rang once or twice then switched to another line. After two more rings and a long pause, a woman answered, and I relayed Jim's invitation. I heard other phones ringing in the background like it was an office I had just called rather than a home. *Was the woman who answered reading from a script?* I wondered.

On the proposed day, the "suits" arrived again, and Jim took them out to see the newly built "hawk house." Our first mew, like all those we have built since, was simplicity personified. We adhered to the guidelines for size, drainage to allay any problems with moisture retention and mold, an opening for sunlight and air, and perching so the bird has a good view and can be out of the wind. Jim explained all this as he showed the pair around the mew. The pair professed their interest, as they had never seen a mew before—or so they said. Jim commented that other falconers' mews must be vastly superior to ours.

"Oh, no," the "son" blurted out. "Compared to the other mews we have seen, this is a hawk palace!"

The "father" shot a look at the "son," both men clammed up, and they bid hasty good-byes while Jim invited them to attend the coming legislative hearing. We never saw or heard from them again. In fact, after Jim's bill passed, we hardly got any more "gonna get me a para-grine" calls.

CHAPTER 17

Licensed!

Rehabilitators and citizen wildlife watchers alike desire a world that has wild animals in it for the present and for future generations. We feel that by doing something for one individual creature, something positive is being done to protect wildlife as a whole. What's not widely known is that almost all wildlife rehabilitation done in the United States today rests on the shoulders of volunteers. This includes donations of money, time, facilities, or services.

It behooves public officials to cooperate with rehabilitators, as the alternative would be for the officials to take on the task themselves, and, without any exceptions, public agencies involved with the environment and with wildlife management are already stretched beyond their capabilities. At the same time, these agencies are dealing with a mass of laws put into place by people concerned for the welfare of the environment and its wild populations. Navigating between permitting an activity regarding wildlife and staying within the laws of the land is a difficult feat. The onerous permitting process rehabilitators go through is the unavoidable consequence.

For us, acquiring the necessary documentation for the rehabilitator's permit went at a frenetic pace. A fellow rehabilitator volunteered the use of her flight cage. Phone calls were made to local veterinarians to ask if they would serve as our vet reference and provide medical assistance. I set up an appointment to meet the veterinarian who returned a call and left with his signed letter clutched tightly in my hand.

I called Mike Cox, director of the Vermont Institute of Natural Science Raptor Center. Mike had seen us through some critical periods with our birds, and I had transferred to him the red-tailed hawk he maintained as a falconry bird. I asked Mike to provide a letter, and when it came, not only was it a glowing report of our experience and worthiness to rehabilitate, but in it Mike also offered several types of assistance, so a number of requirements were satisfied at once.

Silk Farm Audubon Center's Ruth Smith quickly fulfilled our request for a letter. Dave Erler fired off a letter from the Squam Lakes Natural Science Center. With amazing speed, documentation for the federal permit was compiled, but we still had some objectives to complete.

Although the federal government has downlisted the peregrine falcon from endangered to threatened, New Hampshire at that time maintained it on its own endangered species list. The peregrine is held in special esteem by our state wildlife officials because when the decline of the species in North America was recognized, New Hampshire held the only nesting pair located east of the Mississippi River.

A state rehabilitator application with its pages of requirements and instructions was rushed to us from the Fish and Game Department, and I set to work completing it. The most important requirement was a premises visit by the local Fish and Game conservation officer (C.O.) followed by a written recommendation from the officer. My heart sank. It was bad enough to be asking our friends for letters. To have to ask for a C.O. was another thing.

Some states may call them game wardens, but conservation officers in New Hampshire are accorded special status. They enforce the laws governing hunting and fishing as well as many other outdoor recreation and conservation matters. When people get themselves into trouble out in the wilds, conservation officers are called upon to rescue them.

C.O.s are often alone in isolated localities when they work. There is risk involved because lawbreakers sometimes go to murderous lengths to avoid detection or capture. Our local C.O., John Sampson, could have come straight out of the Old West. I had to know him quite a while before I learned he could smile. Always polite, always correct, he is a rigidly "by-the-book" officer. Sampson is someone you would want to have on your side and never be on his wrong side. Asking him to come by for a visit would take courage. I was not sure I could summon enough bravery.

We first met John when he came to inspect our falconry facilities after we moved to his jurisdiction. Thereafter, we could expect an annual return visit from him, "just to check things." A couple years later, John had to plan a meeting for his fellow officers, and he asked if he could hold the meeting at our place so we could give a presentation about falconry. I spoke about the inspection of falconry mews and equipment. The group then quizzed my husband about hunting with falcons and hawks. John Sampson wore such an inscrutable look on his face when I set out cookies and lemonade, I wondered whether he was pleased or irritated. I was certain, though, he had appreciated the program. I figured I could lean on that when I made my bid for a special visit.

When I got him on the phone to launch into my dual request, I heard a quick intake of breath before he explained how busy he was. It was mid-April, the traditional opening of the fishing season. Large numbers of fishermen would be on the lakes, streams, and ponds, and all of their licenses would require checking.

"Perhaps we could schedule this over milk and cookies, Nancy," he said with a chuckle, and I knew I was being told I would get his earliest free moment. Sergeant Sampson had just rearranged his priorities so that a V.I.P. (Very Important Peregrine) could be accommodated.

This might have also been due to the fact that Jim and I had handled a wildlife problem for him long before when a homeowner had called him regarding a young great horned owl sitting on her back deck. John called us and local rehabilitator Maria Colby to help him. We squeezed into Maria's car and headed to the property. When we got there, we became acutely aware that the place reeked of skunk.

Raptors have wonderful sight capabilities but, with the exception of carrion eaters such as condors and vultures, their sense of smell is almost nil. This makes nocturnally active prey such as skunks a great target for owls. Young raptors find meals can be few and far between. A juvenile owl that killed a skunk would not leave until it had eaten all it could. There was the young great horned owl, perched in a small tree overlooking the deck and the dead skunk.

Jim, John, Maria, and I all looked at one another. No one moved a muscle or spoke. Finally my husband strode over to the skunk. He carried the dead, smelly critter away from the house, across the yard, and into a meadow. The great horned owl followed him. When Jim reached a downhill slope, he gave a heave and the skunk sailed into the meadow with the owl closely gliding after it. Problem solved. Except Jim now reeked of skunk, too. We squeezed back into Maria's car, holding our noses for the ride home. After Jim's selfless action, Sergeant Sampson may have felt indebted to the "civilian" who had handled his "wildlife problem."

In the midst of gathering documentation for the permit, a call came from an Audubon biologist named Chris Martin. If any person in our state deserves the title "Mr. Peregrine," it's him. Chris coordinates the efforts in New Hampshire to monitor the nest sites, band the youngsters, and record the data. He is deeply concerned with all things having to do with peregrines and has kept us abreast of matters pertaining to the wild peregrine population. He called to voice his approval of our planned rehab efforts, to offer assistance, and to tell us his own peregrine news.

Turns out, Chris was having a "peregrine spring" of his own. There were thirteen active nest sites in our state that nesting season, and, for the first time, one of them was in an urban location. The nest box placed on the New Hampshire Building, one of Manchester's tallest, was holding four precious eggs which were due to begin hatching, appropriately, on Mother's Day. The building was where Jim had worked until his company relocated his office to Boston. Chris knew how excited we would be at the prospect of young falcons fledging from that building's man-made "cliff ledges."

Chris was also friends with federal biologist Michael Amaral, and together they climbed mountain ledges to check up on each year's crop of New Hampshire peregrines. "Michael says he banded the injured per-egrine up on Holt's Ledge in 1999," I told Chris.

"Well, I helped him climb the cliff!" Chris burst out with a laugh. I invited him to come see the falcon as soon as he could.

Chris, Michael, Dave Erler, and Jim and I are only a few of the many people who take the welfare of peregrines seriously. When the decline in peregrine numbers was noted by falconers and became national news, this raptor became America's poster child for the endangered species programs of our nation. One major cause proved to be the widely used insecticide DDT. Another was the lack of legislation to protect our North American birds and preserve their habitats. The idea that our continent was so polluted as to cause such a strikingly beautiful bird to disappear took hold and lent credence to cleaning up our environment, bestowed power to and increased the scope of protective legislation of our natural resources and wildlife, and gave rise to conservation groups.

The peregrine's special aura is borne from its legend-laced history as a falconry bird, and from its majestic command of the skies. That it is the fastest living creature doesn't hurt either. As difficult as the prospect of helping the injured Holt Ledge peregrine might appear, in the minds of Chris, Michael, Dave, Jim, and me, the effort was assuredly worthwhile.

There were other preparations to do besides assembling paperwork. The mini-mew had to be retrieved, scrubbed down, and aired. This small, two-and-a-half-foot-high portable chamber had been purchased from another falconer a few years prior. It has proven invaluable whenever we have an ailing bird in need of quiet confinement. Keeping the peregrine in the mini-mew would give us time to evaluate its readiness to be perched on a block perch of normal height.

At least once a year we check over and replace worn-out anklets, jesses, and bells. This time we'd need to add equipment specially sized for the wild male peregrine and the young female due to arrive from the breeder. Jim and I put our heads together over the catalogues from Northwoods and Mike's Falconry Supplies, the falconer's equivalents of the Sears and Roebuck "wishbook." We pored over the pages, many of which offer the same item, but in sizes ranging from the tiny (male kestrel) to the immense (female golden eagle). Size varies according to the species of raptor and also by sex, as female raptors are larger than their male counterparts. We wrote out the order to newly outfit each of our birds with anklets, bells, jesses, and a tail-guard for Jim's goshawk, before adding special, removable anklets for the rehab peregrine, ones that could be taken off without having to be cut on release day.

We also ordered a supply of quail from a game farm. Falcons, as a wise master falconer told me once, require "high-octane fuel." And the fellow with injured tissue to rebuild would benefit from the richness of the quail, as would the young, unfledged peregrine coming from the breeder. Fifty pounds of "high test" would set us back about two hundred dollars.

By now letters and affidavits were arriving. I put in another call to John Sampson about his visit, and at the same time made an offer to write the letter for his signature. Shortly afterward, John found time in his schedule, and I had cookies waiting for him.

The day came when I was able to assemble every required document. The lot went into a large Postal Service Express Mail envelope with a return envelope enclosed as well. Three days later our federal rehabilitation permit came rocketing back in the envelope. We could now begin plans to start working with this peregrine!

The clock began ticking off the final moments before Michael Amaral planned to deliver the peregrine. Then disaster struck with a spring snowstorm. The heavy, wet snowfall downed a large limb in the yard, and my husband wrenched his back trying to move it. Within two days, Jim could barely walk. X-rays revealed a severely compressed disc but, fortunately, no ruptures. Like the peregrine due to arrive any moment, he needed rehabilitation.

There was one chair in the living room that afforded Jim some comfort. My two-year-old pointer, Stormy, and I were booked for five full days with one of the best pointing dog trainers in the country, so Jim was going to be stuck at home by himself. The injured peregrine could not have come at a better time. Now Jim had something to take his mind off his pain.

CHAPTER 18

Meet a Bird Named N-Z

On May 7, Michael Amaral and the injured peregrine arrived. As we took the falcon from Michael's vehicle, I asked if the bird had a name. At the question, this federal biologist looked at me sternly. "Rehab birds don't get names, Nancy. It's to keep people from becoming too attached. Anyone handling a bird or animal that's going to be released needs to stay detached."

"Yes, I understand, Michael," I countered. "But asking Jim if 'the wild peregrine in rehab' needs to be fed is kind of a mouthful."

"It is called N-Z," Michael allowed himself to smile. "It's for his band. See?" He pointed to the wide federal band around the falcon's leg, a strip of green and black over galvanized metal with the large letters *N* and *Z* clearly imprinted. When a peregrine is banded, the color combination indicates the year of banding and the sex of the bird, while the letters identify the individual. These are usually read from long distances by biologists and bird-watchers utilizing spotting scopes and strong binoculars.

Within a short time the falcon was removed from the carrier. He was then "cast," which means gently restrained so his feet and legs could be safely handled and equipped with removable anklets and jesses. His new life sharing a house with two humans had commenced. We wanted to win his trust quickly and to overcome the memories of pain and fear he had felt while being doctored in the healing process.

The bird wounded me when he was still agitated from being handled while Jim carefully fit the soft, kangaroo-leather anklets above the bands on each of his legs. Afterwards, as I lifted him to the glove, his head snaked over to strike my bare right hand. Peregrines have strong, pointy beaks, and he drove the point on his into the bone of my knuckle. It was a hit-and-run attack; the falcon's head snapped back as quickly as it had struck. He glared at me. The injury was no larger than a pinhole, but blood welled up. I looked closely at the beak that had assaulted me. The shaping and sharpening were precise. The beak itself was dark and lustrous. Any falconer would be proud to have maintained a falcon as well as this fellow had maintained himself in the wild. *We are dealing with perfection here*, I said to myself in awe.

The falcon's lightning attack happened as I was placing him into the mini-mew. My ungloved hand as I exchanged leashes gave him an opportunity he took without hesitating. Once the leashes were changed, I put on my glove and set the angry bird on it. Within an hour my hand was throbbing inside the gauntlet.

The early stages of "manning," or taming, are never pacifying to a bird of prey. In falconry, we are only ever able to teach a raptor two basic things: 1) that we will provide food on a given signal, and 2) we will not hurt the bird. Almost everything else is a matter of the raptor's instincts.

The bird's first time upon the glove was an important step in the process. Initially the urge to flee caused N-Z to struggle to launch off the glove repeatedly. I had hoped to keep this to a minimum to reduce the strain on the healing wing. The peregrine persisted for a short while and then ceased. He sat stalwartly upon the glove, not yielding, not liking it, but with dignity and calmness. The wing injury did not seem to hinder the falcon's bating, although the droop worsened as soon as he tired the weakened wing. After I felt he had sat long enough on the glove to realize that I would not hurt him, I perched him upon the falcon block set up in our living room and moved away to give him some peace.

Now I removed my falconry glove with relief. Where the falcon had punctured me, the palm was red and swollen. Where his beak had drilled my knuckle was raised and sore. I was looking at what boded to become two dandy infections. During my falconry career I had been footed or pierced by talons and bit numerous times, both by our tame birds and by birds from the wild. Hand scrubbing, disinfecting, and periodic applications of topical antibiotic quelled the small infections, just as these latest ones would heal, although it had happened that deep gashes from talons would sometimes require a visit to the clinic for a shot of antibiotic.

Later that day, I put N-Z away in the mini-mew where it had been ensconced in the center hallway of our old house. A dinner of quail had been left for him, and he did not take long to eat it. What would come next would be days of Jim working his falconer magic to calm and steady N-Z to being handled.

Any wrong move when manning can exacerbate the stress felt by a wild raptor being held. The point is to reassure the bird that the glove is a place of safety and the human wearing it means no harm. Thanks to his own injury, Jim Cowan, the most knowledgeable falconer in New Hampshire, had hours to spend working with this wild peregrine.

CHAPTER 19

The Dance Begins

The following week was a busy one for me. Each morning I was up early, dressed, and bundling Stormy into the dog crate in my Jeep so we could head to "pointer school." Every day was full of learning, training, and practice in a field at the Timberdoodle Club, which was familiar territory because of the falconry demonstrations Jim and I had done there. Stormy and I came home bone-tired and happy every night.

Jim would tell me about his day with N-Z as I fixed dinner. I had little energy for more than a hot bath after dinner, followed by reading over the documents and paperwork that came with the bird. The records on the peregrine made for interesting reading. I now had the names of the people who found the falcon and brought it to the Squam Lakes Natural Science Center. One evening I called one of those men and added the details he shared to the medical case history.

The bird was found "nested on the snowbank" by two state highway maintenance workers driving over a shore road along a lake. As they passed the raptor, the men did a double take, stopped their vehicle, then backed up a bit. They got out and approached the falcon. It tried to fly off but could not manage more than a few yards out onto the lake ice. A chase ensued, and finally, exhausted, the falcon lay still for the humans to pick it up. They brought it straightway to the Squam Lakes Center. The date was March 27, 2001.

Dave Erler had added data to the center's animal record forms Michael Amaral brought down with the falcon. The center staff assumed the wing injury was from a car strike. The medical description read, "Left wing broken—radius close to elbow joint affected (broken?), as well. Large amount of swelling, small wound." The falcon was transported to a local animal hospital, where the wound was flushed and cleansed and the bird was given fluids and antibiotics. Surgery to repair the break revealed a dislocation instead. The wing joint was carefully relocated and wrapped to immobilize it for four weeks. Ten days after the surgery, the bird returned to the clinic to be anesthetized so the sutures could be removed and the wing inspected. The veterinarian decided not to rewrap the healing wing, but instead gave the center staff instructions to house it in small quarters to prohibit much movement.

I compared the written case history with the details from Dave and with the area description from Chris Martin, who had inspected the site where the bird was found. Via telephone, Chris and I theorized as to how the falcon got hurt. There was no feather damage, which usually happens with a car strike. There were no large wounds or scrapes. There was, on the very top of his cere (the nostril area above the beak), a small dark spot, either a bruise or an old scab, that looked like the bird had taken a blow there.

Although the car-strike theory was logical in respect to where the falcon was first seen, it was unsubstantiated. Chris felt it would be surprising if more than three vehicles a day used the road around the lake in March. Perhaps this peregrine was the victim of an attack by another bird of prey. The wound could have been caused by a talon, and the dislocation by a

Jim's hawk became accustomed to my sled team leader, Inga, when she and I accompanied the pair on long hikes during the training process.
NANCY COWAN

Tabasco served as my apprentice bird, as he had for Jim.
MARGARET YOUNG

There was never any doubt Injun was the senior member of our partnership, but when he flew, my heart flew with him.
KEN WILLIAMS

The peregrine named Lass was not averse to enjoying a bath on a sunny day in late February.
KEN WILLIAMS

At the beginning, N-Z's wing injury caused a noticeable droop of the wing.
NANCY COWAN

My big female Harris's hawk, Jazz, was one of the best hunters I have flown.
DON HIMSEL

Teaching the falcon to accept the hood with grace and calmness is a necessary part of training peregrines.
DON HIMSEL

With the dog working ahead in search of the scent of a game bird, the falconer tries to place her hawk in a good position to chase when quarry is flushed.
DON HIMSEL

Following flights, Crash would end by finishing her meal on my glove.
JOANN O'SHAUGHNESSY

Ready to be released, Crash had just finished a large meal and was surprised I was asking her to fly again.
JOANN O'SHAUGHNESSY

Flying 3-D, the young goshawk, was an education in how fast and how high-strung accipiters are.
MARIKO YAMASAKI

I felt like the luckiest falconer alive to have a hawk as good a hunter as Jazz to work over a pointer as talented as Stormy.
NANCY BERGENDAHL

Jim often handles Banshee, our school's peregrine, when we exhibit her at events and demonstrations.

LAURA MURPHY, ADA CAMP CAREFREE

blow from above. It was possible this falcon was going about his normal, everyday routine when he was hurt. I did not want to think his injuries had come about because he frequented a roadside to hunt. If so, he was not likely to change his habits, dooming him to a swift end or further injury if he was released back into the wild.

My five-day pointer class ended, and Jim was finally able to endure the long commute to his office. The days had warmed; spring was turning into summer. It was time to start working with the wild peregrine. I did not want to delay since we were "on the clock." Rehabbers are allowed only ninety days to evaluate and condition birds for release or to decide they can't be released. A non-releasable bird must be turned over to a licensed educator or educational institution to live out its life in captivity, or it must be euthanized. Rehabilitators can petition for another ninety days. N-Z's rehab period would be up in early August, an ideal time for release, as the weather and availability of prey species are most beneficial. Ninety days beyond that would put his release in the month of November, not an ideal time for a number of reasons.

I was amazed at how much my husband had accomplished with manning. N-Z could now be picked up and carried without fussing or bating. His wing had strengthened during his time in the mini-mew, so he could move to his own quarters. It was important for him to start living outside, as it was time for the new young peregrine to arrive. She would take his place indoors, and by the time N-Z was rehabilitated, she would move to the mew he presently inhabited.

Living loose, or "free lofted" as falconers call it, in a building with perches at various heights, a comfortable sleeping shelf at the highest point, and a large sunny window would give N-Z some limited exercise to get him ready for the time he would start flying free. If Jim had not done such a good job of manning this falcon, free lofting would not have been possible. Flying madly about the mew, crashing into walls or perches, would have undone all the healing, surgery, and care N-Z had received.

Although N-Z did not welcome my presence in the mew, he stood quietly and did not bate or try to escape whenever I entered and reached out to pick up his jesses to attach the swivel and leash. Thanks to Jim's efforts, N-Z and I were ready to begin building the partnership a free-flying raptor and its falconer share.

One of the reasons I love peregrines so much is the effect training and handling them has on time. It stops, or at least it slows considerably. This is probably because the falconer has to focus completely on the training. Because rushing any part of the training may mar the falcon, I prepared myself at the onset to single-mindedly devote myself to the project at hand.

Let me confess right here my initial experiences in training and flying falcons were not all that serendipitous. My first was a lanner falcon given to me by our friend Tom Ricardi seven years before. As well as being a falconer and rehabilitator, Tom is a propagator, or breeder. He kept a pair of lanners from which he produced offspring, but his male had died sometime before. The female he gave me was its mate. She was not young and had, in fact, stopped laying eggs before the death of the male. We perched the falcon in our kitchen. The first thing to do in manning was to get her accustomed to humans again. Although it was rumored she had started life as a falconry bird, her years in the breeding chamber left her extremely wild. We put her perch next to the trash can, which ensured she would get considerable experience with the comings and goings of her human housemates.

Lanner falcons are not native to North America. They were discovered by Europeans when they traveled to the Middle East during the Crusades. The knights took pairs of these small, handsome falcons home for breeding and to be used in falconry. Lanners don't have the size, power, or ambition for sizable quarry and are usually put after smaller birds as prey. Lanners don't have the blistering speed of the peregrine and they don't climb high into the sky; however, the compact flights of these stylish beauties suit them very well in the tight spaces typical of the New England countryside, and their greed, or inability to turn away from opportunities for food, enables falconers to train them rapidly.

Once she got used to our moving to and from the kitchen trash can, the lanner began to trust us. And she liked the meals she was fed on the glove. Soon she was greeting us when we approached. She'd cackle with delight at the prospect of dinner, which resulted in the fond nickname we gave her: "Mrs. Chicken."

Before long, Mrs. Chicken was ready to be tried in flight. We took her to our backyard and attached a thin line called a creance, which allows us to test fly a bird just trained. Jim held her while I called to her from across the yard. It was a perfect training flight. She left Jim's glove on the call, came toward me, passed in a semicircle, and came back to my glove. Her textbook training flight encouraged us, so we next tried something more ambitious—no strings attached!

Jim stood with the lanner at our driveway while I walked fifty yards away across the cul-de-sac in the subdivision in which we lived. Again, Mrs. Chicken responded promptly to the call, but this time she did not rise into the air. She came at the height of Jim's glove and actually lost height as she approached. Moreover, she was laboring hard by the time she reached me and could barely make it up to my glove. She sat on my glove, panting and barely able to focus on the tidbit it held. Jim and I called it quits for the day. A question loomed over us: Was this bird out of condition from years of non-flight, or was she just too old to start over in flying? I got my answer on her next and final flight.

I often refer to falcons, all falcons, as not being the brightest of creatures. Confront falcons with something that overwhelms them in any way, and their usual reaction is a meltdown. I never see them figure out situations with the brain power possessed by Harris's hawks. But never say never, right?

Mrs. Chicken absolutely astonished me when I took her out to see how she would fly after being rested. Our backyard was a quiet place and a small space in which to work, so I placed her perch near the stairs to our outdoor deck and walked a short distance away before I called her. At the sound of the whistle, she jumped off her perch, turned her back to me, and started up the stairs to the deck, hopping up each one. I was dumbfounded. The deck stood about fourteen feet off the ground. Mrs. Chicken eventually reached the top stair, negotiated it in a final hop, then tootled across the deck to the edge, where she spread her wings and launched herself to glide down to my glove.

It was perhaps the most inventive stoop any falcon has ever achieved. She deserved a medal for the performance. But the result was it showed me I was asking this sweet little falcon to do something beyond her ability, and so we officially retired Mrs. Chicken. She spent the rest of her days with us (which numbered not much more than a year) eating her dinners and occasionally being exhibited if we did a program. She was a hit at every event because she was as endearing as she was beautiful. As far as my career in flying falcons was concerned, I had to wait until the day came that I had a peregrine.

Sometime after the demise of Mrs. Chicken, I was fortunate to be given a peregrine, a failed breeder-bird, from a falcon propagator in the Midwest. She was a beauty: large, regal, and in all ways a perfect reflection of what was called in the Middle Ages "the falcon-gentle," meaning "best of all falcons." She was an imprint, meaning she was raised from the time she hatched to relate to humans. This is commonly done with falcons that are to be used in captive breeding programs. It also produces especially loyal and quiet falcons for falconry. An added bonus was she had been trained as a falconry bird by a master (and masterful) falconer prior to her unsuccessful career as a breeder.

This peregrine, "Lass" as I called her, was the epitome of imprinting and training done right, but there was an entirely new set of rules to which I had to become accustomed. Lass leapt into the great void of my ignorance to teach them to me. The first time I entered her mew with a tidbit of food was the last time I entered the mew of an imprinted raptor with food on my glove. My hands were instantly bound together by her locked grasp of the wristbands of my sweatshirt, and I had to yell loudly to get Jim's attention so he could free me.

From there I moved boldly to my first flight with the big peregrine. The lure I was using had a large spindle for a handle. I became so excited about calling her down that I cast the lure straight up and stood gazing upwards to see the outcome, which came all too soon. The handle fell back along the trajectory of my toss and whacked me a good one across my nose and eye socket. As I stood swaying, dizzy, and dazed, Lass sweetly fluttered down upon the lure which had in the meantime landed beside me. My first flight-with-a-peregrine memento was a black eye that lasted about a week. On the plus side was the enduring and very practical understanding that it is not good to stand under the spot from which you threw the lure, especially a lure with a large spindle handle.

There were many more lessons I learned in the years before Dave Erler's call about the injured peregrine. And, true to my start, I always seemed to learn the hard way.

CHAPTER 20

Can He Fly?

The falcon circled above, her path a perfect elliptical shape. Down, turn, back, around, turn. Over and over. Whenever my husband wanted to change her flight pattern or bring her in closer, he would slip the lure from out of his coat pocket and give it just one swing before re-pocketing it. The appearance of the lure, however brief, would turn his falcon right back towards him. When he tossed it up, she dove down, snatching it out of the air to land gently on the ground. Watching Jim with Tater was a wonderful lesson for me as I moved past my apprenticeship. I learned why "wedded to the lure" was a trait falconers desired in their falcons.

In falconry, hawks are known as "birds of the glove" and falcons are referred to as "birds of the lure." That's because a hawk can swoop down to land and perch upon the glove. After initial training, when a falcon is flying in its normal fashion of stooping faster than a NASCAR driver, calling it to the glove will surely result in injury to the falcon or the falconer. For falcons flying too high to hear a whistle, the upswing of a lure is a strong attention-getter.

Flying lures can look like a bird in flight or like a football someone ran over with a steamroller. Lures have strings for tying on small bits of food, cords by which they are swung, and sometimes handles on the end of the cords. The best lures are small enough to easily tuck into a game pocket, yet large enough to be the size of something the raptor might catch. When calling the falcon down from the heavens, a falconer swings it so the lure is on the rise as the falcon flies at it. This is called "serving the lure." It is the most important tool a falconer has when flying a falcon.

In the light of day, the eye of a raptor is extremely powerful at discerning small objects at great distances. Added to the recognition that the lure carries food is the fact that it swings into the air much as a bird in flight rises from the ground. Raptor eyes are sensitized to detect prey in motion. Once the falcon is accustomed to the lure through proper training, you have a foolproof callback. Tater, trained with the lure from the beginning, reacted exactly as her wild instincts dictated she should to an easy food opportunity coupled with the enticement of prey movement.

N-Z's training would follow the same course as Tater's. The first step is to introduce the bird to the lure, so he is not frightened of it. This is usually accomplished in several days of feeding the falcon meals tied to the lure. While he is sitting tethered to a perch, the falconer approaches, blows the whistle, swings the lure laden with a tidbit, and allows it to drop within the falcon's reach.

N-Z had already become accustomed to eating from the lure. He welcomed every meal, so when his dinner came swinging at him for the first time, this avian hunter rose from the perch to snatch the lure out of the air with both feet. I was thrilled we were off to a good start so quickly. N-Z's finely honed hunting skills and his appetite for dinner were going to be valuable assets during his training.

Training was interrupted, however, on May 30, when I made a trip to Manchester Airport to meet a passenger flying in from Idaho. I arrived as the plane was landing. My traveler would not be off-loaded until the human passengers and their luggage were unloaded at the main terminal. It seemed like hours before the desk clerk brought out an animal carrier and set it on the counter. I could not wait a second longer to look at my new charge. I asked for a pair of scissors to break the cable ties holding the door closed. Carefully I cracked open the carrier door and peeked in.

Seemingly composed mostly of white fluff with eyes of obsidian and a huge beak that made the bird appear like a wizened old elf, it stared back at me without making a sound. What I was looking at resembled the kitchen witch dolls that were popular when I was a girl. Within a heartbeat, I was in love and named her on the spot. "Witch" and I started for home and at the same time began a journey leading me to both exhilaration and despair.

Having a very young falcon in the house is like having a baby in your care. Meals have to be supplied often and plentifully. The eyass needs a safe space which does not stay clean for long, so a large box with high sides was procured and lined with newspaper that was changed often. But one doesn't box up a baby. Young things need to have stimulation and to bond with their caretakers. So the baby got lots of attention and regular intervals of running about the floor inside or the grass outside. Like other babies, Witch had to be kept out of trouble and protected while she was enjoying these outings. I was busy taking care of a bouncing baby peregrine growing by leaps and bounds whose feathers were suddenly beginning to poke through the white fluff. As the feathers grew, the fluff got shed. The inside of my house screens became covered with down. Witch grew large enough and strong enough to begin scaling to the top of her box. It was time for her to wear anklets and be tethered to the perch she could now jump to and from with ease.

During all this growth and change, I was reading books on training falcons. In one, written by Witch's breeder, the author pointed out that the more there was for the developing young bird to watch, the better.

Once Witch grew large enough to be perched, she loved sitting inside the front screen door to watch the traffic go down our street. Close the door for inclement weather or because we were leaving the house, and she would vocalize her disapproval vehemently. I resorted to a suggestion in the book by perching her in front of the TV, which performed "eyass-sitting duty" for the young falcon.

N-Z's training was proceeding all the while. With the demands of a job, household duties, and raising Witch, I was kept racing. By now I had started lure training with Witch, too. After I finished working with N-Z, I would fill a bath pan with water and set it beside him. He would bathe and preen in the sunshine as I settled in for the session with Witch. It was an idyllic way to spend part of a summer day, but devoting time to two birds meant the rest of my hours were crowded beyond capacity. Even so, taking the utmost care over every phase of training was a respite from the hectic life I was leading.

We were working on something that builds trust, and the lure was an important part of this procedure. We had already established that whenever I showed N-Z food on the glove and whistled, he would jump to my fist from his perch. N-Z was rising from the perch to the length of his leash to catch the lure in the air. Having caught it, he would devour the portion of his meal tied to it. At this stage of the training I would hover nearby as he ate, kneeling to offer my glove which held the best and favorite part of the dinner, a quail breast. This would bring him jumping to the glove. As N-Z fed on the glove, I would reach down quietly and with utmost discretion remove the lure to the game pocket of my vest. The unwritten contract between a falconer and a falcon is that the human will never steal food or the lure. Taking either before a raptor has given it up constitutes (to the raptor) a theft of the greatest proportions.

Day after day N-Z and I followed this ritual until I could approach him as he ate on the lure and, while he still was feeding from it, reach below his tail and gently pick up each jess and attach my hunting leash to the swivel ring. Then I would offer the glove with a morsel of quail breast and have him jump up, and I would pocket the lure as described. This training plays a huge role in flying a raptor free and is the method of recovering the bird when it has taken game.

This positive reinforcement / consistent training part of lure training pays huge dividends when your falcon has landed and you need to retrieve him. The falcon demonstrates total trust if he allows you to approach and to handle him when he is on something he caught. Especially with a rehab falcon in recovery for injuries, retrieving him from his conditioning flights was mandatory. N-Z took to this training remarkably well. A falcon with the least doubt about the human approaching him will "mantle," or spread his wings over his food, hiss, raise the crest of feathers at the back of his head and neck, and otherwise make it plain the person is encroaching too closely. Any closer after the warning will earn the falconer a painful "footing" on the falconer's fingers. If the training is not done well, the falcon will not be waiting around on the lure at all but will be flailing madly at the end of his leash, trying to escape. If he were loose, he would be gone for good.

N-Z exhibited incredible laissez-faire about the whole thing. I wish I could say it was because of my formidable skill as a falconer, but the truth was N-Z, like a trucker at a diner, was just plain tickled pink food came so easily. He had been making his way in the world for two years, and no predator has an easy life. Now he had dinner served to him, and he was downright appreciative. The one thing he didn't tolerate was if I had been too invasive in my handling of him. If, for example, I was clumsy and touched his tail as I reached under for a jess, he would fix his eye upon me, and I knew he was keeping score. Retribution would usually come after I had returned him to the mew and was removing his leash and swivel. At the very last minute, those black eyes would stare at me and then he would reach over and bite me. It was not an attack, but a tribute to be exacted for being too familiar with royalty. Eventually I got used to it.

Flight training started with the old jump-to-the-glove-on-the-whistle routine N-Z had mastered. Raptors do not come to the glove for a reward, nor do they feel gratitude for a treat. Rather, they see all food as theirs—only they must get to it. By winning the bird's trust so the glove is an accepted place to eat safely, the falconer is making himself the path to an easy meal. Birds of prey are programmed like all other predators to seek an easy opportunity for food when it is presented. Far from being masters of the falcon, all of us who fly raptors make use of the birds' instinctive acceptance of this situation. However, this works only if the raptor is inclined to eat. This means the energy-saving falcon is going to fly when he is ready to hunt, so the falconer must learn what a bird's "flying weight" should be.

Flying weight is a normal, healthy weight. It is what it would mean to the average person, coming indoors on a crisp fall day after an energetic hike to find a favorite meal already on the table. At that moment food seems like a good idea. This is the way raptors feel when they are at "flying weight." It is not absolute hunger or starvation. One way we recognize it is by watching how avid the raptor is in response to food. To be able to judge a correct flying weight takes study.

All of our birds are weighed before we work with them, and this pattern was established with N-Z as well. Because he was healing from an injury, I always allowed for him to be a bit on the heavy side. When it was mealtime for N-Z, he was weighed, perched, and then called to the glove. Soon I was carrying him to different places while tying off the leash to my glove so I could distance myself farther and farther away. When I got as far as the leash would allow, the jump had become a flight.

At that point it was time to switch to the creance line. With this thin cord attached now to N-Z's swivel, I would perch him and walk some distance away, like ten feet, and then call him. Next we would try twenty feet. We did that several times over the next few days. N-Z always responded perfectly, as well as or better than any other bird I had trained. This fellow looked forward to every meal. It was hard to find him at a point where he was too sated to not feel an urgency to come to me. For N-Z, every call was the dinner bell, and he responded promptly.

Knowing I had four thousand years of falconry practices behind what I was doing with this beautiful specimen from the wild, the response of N-Z to my signals was no surprise. Still, when I paused to think about the absolute freedom the air provided him, it thrilled me that a wild bird and I could come to a synchronization of purpose so quickly. The image of N-Z, wild and once again a master of the air, was a vision I held every moment I spent working with him.

Besides evaluating his readiness to return to the wild, I was watching his injured wing very carefully. When he had arrived, there was a pronounced wing droop. By now, N-Z's wing had improved. He was beginning to favor it less. At times he would tuck it up properly so by appearance there was nothing wrong, but most of the time he carried the wing with a slightly detectable droop. If he tired from jumping up or down from his perch, or if I called him on the creance more than twice, the injured wing would take on a pronounced droop. The wing droop was an obstacle that was slowing down our training schedule.

Every time I held him on the glove and his wing began to droop, I would lightly run my finger down the forward edge of the wing, causing him to draw it up tightly to his body. I did this over and over, hoping this repetitive motion would help to strengthen his damaged muscles and ligaments without putting undue stress upon the wing, but it earned me a bite every day at the end of our sessions because, as I said, N-Z always kept score. The biting did not faze me, but my initial thoughts on how this bird's injury was in some ways worse than a break returned to haunt me. If N-Z had been one of my falconry birds, I would have put him up for at least a year to rest his badly strained wing. I would have let him rest, eat quail, and rest some more. I would have started a very conservative conditioning program only after I felt time and rest had accomplished all that was possible in healing the wing. But ninety days was all I had.

I cursed the ninety-day rule. The alternative—deciding that N-Z was not releasable—was even less palatable. I wanted this bird back in the air, and I wanted his wing strong enough for him to survive on his own. Could both of my wishes come true?

CHAPTER 21

Airborne

The day of reckoning came. I was confident N-Z would come at the call, but I was less confident about how he would go about it. Would it be a direct, straight-arrow flight, or would he take himself up to a tree and then swoop down? Would he do a "fly by," meaning would he make a pass and then buttonhook back from the opposite direction to come to my glove? I took him up to the small field above the house where I had been flying him on the creance. To N-Z it probably seemed like any other training day, but my heart was pounding as I knelt to set him on the perch in the middle of the field.

Deliberately I removed the leash and the swivel from his jesses, then rose and walked carefully away, afraid that one wrong move would set him in motion before I was ready. As I walked with my back to him, I slipped a quail leg out of my pocket and between the thumb and forefinger of my glove. I stopped, turned, and raised my gloved hand, but never had a chance to blow the whistle. N-Z was on the move straight to my glove. He came in like a bullet now that he wasn't dragging the weight of the creance line. His second flight assured me he knew he was free. Once he finished the quail leg, I set him again on the perch and stepped back.

There was just a short pause before he launched himself into the air. He circled around me before landing high in the top of a spruce at the edge of the field. I slipped my glove off and pulled the lure loaded with quail meat from my pocket. Giving a whistle, I swung the lure once before tossing it to the ground between us. He was down in a flash. As he gorged on quail, I knelt beside him to slip my hand behind his legs to attach the snap of my hunting leash to each jess. We sat there for a while in the pleasant, sunny afternoon. Both of us were pleased with the outcome of the first day of free flight.

For most of that week, N-Z and I did flight training in the small field. I would perch him and step away. When I stopped and turned to face him, he would shift from foot to foot once or twice and then he was off. Every day the flights got better, longer, faster. But for a falcon, he was flying extremely low. By the second day he was nearly at treetop level—too low for a bird that normally does well over a thousand feet and higher in the sky with ease. By the fourth free flight he was weaving in and out of the treetops lining the field at roadside. I would lose sight of him for moments at a time, but his reappearance was something I could count upon.

If N-Z grew tired, he had a favorite limb in a spruce where he would alight to catch his breath. If I saw his wing drooping during one of his stops, I'd pull out the lure and he'd react instantly. I tossed the lure up so he could hit it at the apex of its ascent and ride it down. My heart throbbed faster in unison with his wing beats during each flight. Time and space ceased to exist. There was only the falcon circling, and in the middle of the circle was me holding down the scrap of earth that was the center of the universe for both of us.

I wanted to share N-Z's progress with Michael Amaral and Chris Martin, the men who had climbed the cliff and banded him as an eyass.

Several days later the two came to watch as I flew him. They were curious about the state of N-Z's drooping wing, so I repeated the flights we had been doing all week. Michael and Chris had seen peregrines fly, but I think this was the first time they had seen one responding to the lure and landing to peacefully eat quail as a human clipped his jesses to her leash. They had cameras ready but remained at a distance, not wanting to frighten N-Z. I told them he was bombproof when eating his dinner. I don't think they believed a wild falcon could be so calm, but N-Z proved my words as they approached. They were pleased with the rehab conditioning we had done so far.

"I have never seen a peregrine flying in such tight surroundings," Michael remarked. Chris nodded in agreement. Michael's words raised a question in my mind: Was I restricting N-Z with my choice of flight area? "Perhaps I should change to a larger field nearby," I offered. This prompted a discussion about transporting N-Z. Fortunately there was a large overlook at the top of our hill with a bigger field in which to work, and it was just a short walk away.

The next week, we trekked to the field on the hilltop. N-Z rode the glove very well. In some places the roadside shoulder was narrow, and I turned my body to shield him from the whoosh of cars and trucks speeding past. We had done this walk many times before. Walking with N-Z was a good way to work at manning, and the balancing upon my glove gave him some mild exercise for his wing droop. On our previous hikes we would often pause at the beautiful vista called the Overlook. The view went for miles, across the Contoocook River valley to the slopes of Riley Mountain to the west. During sunset or when fall has painted the landscape with color, the Overlook is a favorite of photographers and nature lovers. The field rolled downhill, terraced out, and then dropped steeply into the wooded valley. At one side was a grove of tall pines. To the north, Mount Sunapee was visible. To the south, Hedgehog Mountain cut the view of the river valley. Above all was limitless sky. Here N-Z would be free of the cramped boundaries of the small field in which we had been flying.

Not everyone was happy about our plan to fly there. The landowners, our neighbors, were very generous in encouraging me to use the field, but there were at least two tenants who were displeased about N-Z's arrival there. North America's smallest falcon is the kestrel, and a pair of them had nested in the grove at the side of the field. N-Z and I had been the target of a barrage of high-pitched complaints from them during our rest stops at the Overlook. The kestrels were frenetic in their efforts to discourage us, going so far as to swoop down at us with shrill cries. My presence alone would not have caused either of the kestrels to turn a feather, but N-Z's shape instilled instant alarm. The histrionics would eventually subside as the kestrels retreated to the cover of the trees.

Having flown raptors in the Overlook field before, I knew the terrain well and had a plan when I arrived with N-Z for our first flight there. The field was divided roughly into three parts consisting of a lower half and two upper quadrants. An overgrown farm road bounded by stone walls traversed downward near the center. A stone wall cut midway across the width of the field to separate those upper sections from the lower portion. In the higher field the grass was long and dense, which made walking difficult. It was easier to take the center path over the old farm road down to the lower level. The thin soil on the lower half of the field below the wall had little vegetation and walking was easier. There were several large boulders that could be used as perfect take-off spots for the falcon.

It had become our practice for me to perch N-Z, step away, and give one swing to the lure as his take-off signal. I would quickly pocket the lure out of sight while N-Z worked around me in circles. On the first day at the new flying field, I set him on one of the boulders and turned my back. I was as uncertain of what would happen next as I had been on our first flight at the house. Would all this space and air exert a pull to N-Z that my callback could not overcome?

N-Z wasted no time once I flipped the lure out. He started around me, pumping his wings to gain height. Freed from the boundaries of the smaller field, he began making use of the limitless space. He rose higher than I had ever seen him fly and then spread out his circle enormously, zipping out over the river valley and down its length to disappear past where Hedgehog Mountain jutted towards the west. Within moments he crested Hedgehog on his way back. I could tell by his wing beats that this longer, faster flight had tired his injured wing, so I pulled out the lure again and blew the whistle. His circle shortened up to the size of the Overlook field, and as he passed over me, I threw the lure up for him. He landed with it not twenty feet from where I had been standing and began eating the quail tied upon it.

My heart was singing. N-Z had come back even before I had signaled. He was basing his flight around me. Everything had worked perfectly. I barely touched the ground as I walked home with him. However, N-Z's wing was drooping badly. As I walked, I stroked the wing edge and he tucked the wing up. After he had rested and sunned for a bit on his block in the yard, he was carrying the wing much better. I received the obligatory falcon bite as I removed his equipment once back in his mew.

As often as I could, we made the trip up to the Overlook to fly, but it was never as often as I would have liked. With N-Z's regular flights a priority, it was more difficult to fit in time to work with Witch. She had reached a point when the hours of training I devoted to her were critical. She was doing beautifully at rising from her perch to catch a low-slung lure. She allowed me to handle her jesses, to step over her, to move around and about her as she stood eating. Immediately when she finished eating what the lure had held, she looked to me with my outstretched glove waiting.

Unlike N-Z, Witch had been trained to the hood. I have hood-trained older birds successfully, but it is much easier with youngsters like Witch to accustom them to wearing a hood. I began when Witch was still downy. An oversize hood, called a rufter hood, was placed gently on her head just before feeding. At this point she was eating from a dish. As soon as the hood was on her head, I would set out her dish. Then I'd remove the hood gently and, *Voila!* There was her dinner. Instant pleasurable association!

This process of hooding was done religiously for every feeding, so as she grew, Witch never minded wearing a hood. Eventually she was introduced to a hood that was perfectly sized to her head. It was mandatory for Witch to be hood-trained because I travel with my falcons to hunting areas, and this necessitates them riding side by side tethered and perched on a cadge. If the falcons were unhooded, they might hurt one another or become frightened by riding in the car. Or they'd become so excited or agitated, they'd be worn out by the time we reached the hunting fields.

A well-trained falcon will accept a properly fitted hood gracefully. This is known in falconers' parlance as being "good to the hood." Witch had become very accustomed to the hood, which made handling and hooding her very easy. Since the falcon is usually sitting upon the glove while being hooded, the falconer, in order to tighten or loosen the braces (the straps that tighten and loosen the hood), uses her free hand to pull one brace while the matching brace is clasped in her teeth. The falconer's head bobs down and accomplishes this as smoothly as a ballet dancer pivots his prima ballerina. The entire operation resembles a beautiful pas de deux. The act of a falcon sweetly accepting the hood is one of the most beautiful things I know. I took pride and pleasure in the fact that Witch was good to the hood.

When we were done with the day's training, I could not bring myself to hurry away the pleasant hours as the two falcons sunned, bathed, and preened while sitting perched in our yard. Passing traffic, birds flying overhead, and flitting butterflies were entertaining to both birds. To watch these peregrines, lovely and at ease in their surroundings, was more than adequate repayment for the rest of my hectic hours.

Training progressed into the final weeks of July. N-Z's flights at the Overlook were now routine. With every flight he became stronger and faster. My timing at swinging the lure had to be just right since all our flights now ended with N-Z coming down for a pass as I tossed it high into the air. He would hit and bind to it, riding it down to land and feed. Most days we were working in absolute synchronization. Some days, however, things did not go as planned. These were the days I learned lessons about falcons and the flying of falcons.

One such day I climbed the hill on a bright sunny morning, then turned to make the short walk down the pathway at the center of the field to the spot we normally began flying. I set N-Z on our accustomed boulder, stepped away as I pulled out the lure for one swing, and quickly tucked it under my armpit as the falcon rose and began ringing up in increasingly wide circles about me. At that moment a gust of cool, moist wind fanned the back of my neck. I turned to see an enormous black cloud had blown up behind my shoulder. There's an inside joke shared by New Englanders: If you do not care for the weather here, wait five minutes, and it will change. I had been paying attention to N-Z, not to the sky. As I had walked to our spot, this storm had been quickly brewing and was now boiling over the ridge at my back. It was headed straight for us, and within moments the sun was blocked out. Big wet drops began to splash down.

My first reaction was to blow my whistle and swing the lure. I wanted to get N-Z down before the deluge hit. He immediately came back in a tighter circle around me and paused between wing beats to look at me, then took off to circle again. The spattering raindrops increased to a steady shower. He came back and seemed to hover over me fifty feet in the air before making a half-hearted stoop from which he immediately pulled out. On the third circle he cast me a look, then took off for the cover of the big pines, where I saw him land on a high branch sheltered by thickly needled limbs above it. By now I was already as soaked as if someone had emptied a barrel of water over me. I had no desire to become a human lightning rod in the open field, so I decided to sit down. There was nothing to do but wait for the rainstorm to end. I could see N-Z's silhouette perched in the pines. Obviously one of us had enough sense to come in out of the rain, and it wasn't me.

Rather than contemplate how wet I was getting, I thought about what had just happened. N-Z had been responsive to the whistle and to the sight of the lure but had not come down. He had attempted to do so more than once, which indicated a frustration on his part that he could not accomplish what he wanted to do. It worked itself out in my brain as I sat; I realized N-Z had not been able to overcome his instinct not to land in a rainstorm. Of course, it was falcon common sense. If he had become soaked on the ground, how would he have been able to elude some predator or other danger?

The sun shone again, and all across the field and the valley below, steam was rising in the summer's heat. Despite the mist I could see N-Z plainly where he was perched in the pine, but now he was facing in the opposite direction. I saw him bob once or twice and then launch out over the valley. His flight took him past Hedgehog Mountain and out of my sight. I held my breath for a heartbeat or two, but he did not reappear. *Well*, I thought, *N-Z was due to be released in a week or so. He just moved the timetable up a bit.* I had hoped to have a small ceremony for the release, but N-Z had released himself, and I wasn't sorry. If he was ready to go, so be it.

I began climbing the hill along the farm road path, idly swinging the lure as I walked, thinking about the times N-Z and I had flown in this field. About halfway up, I was startled by a sudden noise behind my ear. *Whap!* As I turned, there at my eye level, with the lure firmly grasped in his talons, N-Z sailed past. He was riding the lure like a magic carpet as he hurtled sideways past my face, giving the situation a clownish air of high comedy. N-Z might as well have had a cartoon bubble over his head that said, *Where'd you think you were going without me?* His flight down the valley had not been a departure but had been a "drying out the feathers" run.

I knelt beside where he and the lure had landed and caught up his jesses. I must have worn a smile as wide as the field. In the written rules and unwritten contract of wildlife rehabilitation, the rehabber knows attachment to wild animals is not allowed. N-Z had his own contract, however. The precepts of falconry had built a bond I had not expected. I knew that N-Z, once I cut the bond, would return to his wild state with no difficulty. But in the deepest part of my heart, I realized that the bond I had with such a free and perfect creature was a rare privilege. Soaking wet, smiling like a lunatic, I left the field with the falcon I had brought there.

The ninety days were coming to an end, and it was time to plan N-Z's release. He still had a distinct wing droop, but after a period of rest, it would reset to a normal position. I was not sure how this would affect his life in the wild, but N-Z's performance during flight proved him able to hunt. It was time for him to go. I called every person with a role in his recovery, including the highway workers who had plucked him from the frozen lake and Dave at Squam Lakes Science Center, who had set N-Z's rehab with us in motion, to invite them to the release. Michael Amaral and Chris Martin were invited, too. A few others cleared their schedules to come.

Everyone wanted to see the "star." I got N-Z out to have his photo taken. There was a representative from the local newspaper and a reporter from the *Concord Monitor*. I had decided having the press was a good idea. What if N-Z got into trouble after his release? If people knew there was a recovering peregrine in the area, they would watch out for him.

When the time came to walk to the Overlook, I walked alone with N-Z. A small group trailed some distance behind, and others drove on ahead. The group re-formed at the top of the Overlook while I went down the path to our flying area. Everyone had a perfect view of the action. The reporters followed me partway, settling to sit on the path where they could see and photograph what was about to happen. I had briefed everyone that we would do a normal practice flight. Then, after retrieving N-Z from the lure, I would take a seat on one of the large boulders in the wall to feed him up on quail, gaining time to remove the equipment he wore.

Everything happened just the way I had planned. N-Z made some large circles out over the valley before I called him down with a lure laden with half a quail. As he ate, I retrieved him. By the time I got settled on a big, flat rock, he had finished his half. At that point I deviated from everything we had done in the past by slapping a large quail into my glove. N-Z never hesitated but went straight to work devouring this new prize. He was eating away steadily as I unclipped my hunting leash, pulled out each jess, and began working at the removable anklets one at a time to bare each leg.

By the time I had finished, N-Z was half done with the quail and was becoming very full. He wore only the big, non-removable federal band. He glanced over at me in curiosity but never showed any nervousness about me handling his feet and legs so intimately. I was worried he would be startled and would bate from my glove, as there was nothing holding him to me except his eagerness to finish the quail. I wanted to get both anklets off. They were expensive and could be reused. If he had bated off then, he would have left wearing one or both. Because the grommets were no longer secured by a jess, the anklets encircling his legs would eventually fall off in the wild.

I finished and slipped the anklets into my pocket. All that was left was for him to leave. N-Z, however, was not about to go while there was still quail on the glove. I soaked up the sunshine and the experience of holding this wonderful falcon on my glove for the last time, while N-Z savored every last morsel of his favorite dish. His trust was total and, even though I had altered from our usual course of action, he was satisfied to sit calmly. The snap of the quail bones was audible to the reporters a short distance away. Everyone was waiting in the still summer morning to see what would happen next.

Finally N-Z was done. With the air of a country gentleman finished with an unusually choice repast, N-Z looked up and around. His crop was distended. I knew he was all for settling in a comfortable spot to let the meal digest, but we had an agenda of which N-Z was not aware. By cropping him up so fully, I made sure he was not going to be suffering hunger pangs for at least two days. He would have time to orient himself, to pick a hunting area, and to settle back into his wild existence before there was any urgency to find food. He picked at one tiny bit of red quail meat and then calmly feaked, or rubbed his beak clean, on my glove. I raised my glove on high. Every human witness tensed, waiting for him to explode into the air. Nothing happened.

I brought him down, eye to eye with me. "Time to go, buddy," I said, and raised my glove again. N-Z looked down at me, and though falcon faces are not very expressive, I knew there was a question mark in his eyes. The third time I raised my glove in a thrust upward, and I gave a flick to my wrist. The message to N-Z was very clear: It was time to fly again. He took to the air and began his circles around me. That was the last of him I saw because I purposefully did not look up again. I climbed down from my perch and started out of the field. It was not easy to see my sneakers taking one deliberate step after another because my eyes were swimming with tears. I always cry when bidding good friends adieu. Someone told me long ago it brings bad luck to watch those leaving as they go out of sight. And I certainly wished for N-Z all the good luck in the world.

They told me later that N-Z broke his circling and returned to hover over me as I climbed the path. He paused and, seeing no response from me, made a wider circle, climbing all the while. I thought I saw a raptor shape flitting through the lower clouds hanging over the valley as I reached the highway, but my eyes weren't focusing well. There was only one thing I wanted at the moment. Jim enveloped me in a big hug. "You did good," he said, giving my shoulders a squeeze. The painful lump in my throat melted away as we walked home together.

CHAPTER 22

Flying to Despair

With N-Z now gone, my overbooked schedule opened up, so I could concentrate on Witch. I started her flights in the small field by the house, but it only took one or two times to have me reevaluating my choice of flying areas. Flying Witch was like giving a giddy sixteen-year-old the keys to Dad's Ferrari. I was not sure I could withstand the adrenaline overload as she wove in and around buildings and trees at top speed. Reaching the west side of the field, she flew straight up the middle of Route 149, and I worried she was going to run people off the road by "playing chicken." When my heart rate returned to normal, I knew the next step would be the Overlook.

Flying Witch was completely unlike flying N-Z. She was the first young falcon I had trained and flown myself. Previously I had flown trained adults, then had trained and flown N-Z. The difference between a recuperating seasoned veteran and a youngster raised in captivity was profound. I knew part of the peregrine mystique is its propensity to "push the envelope." While I was trying to keep my sensory overload at a manageable level, Witch was exploring, testing, and stretching every limit of what a peregrine could do.

About ten days after N-Z's release, the phone rang. It was Chris Martin, the Audubon biologist. His tone was not upbeat, and his sentences came out haltingly. I realized he was giving me time to compose myself. Falconers are more aware than anyone that life for raptors is a transitory thing. I was prepared for whatever he had to tell me.

Chris told me that a peregrine had been picked up after being hit by a car. The car-strike had dealt a mortal blow.

"It was N-Z?" I already knew the answer. "How did he get hit by a car? What was he was doing in the road?"

Chris began relating what he had been told. A fellow had come upon a peregrine lying along Route 47. The falcon had been struck by a car and killed. Recognizing it as a peregrine, the man picked it up and brought it to his wife, a teacher at Great Brook School in Antrim. Knowing the Audubon peregrine biologist should be contacted, she took the body to school to keep it in the science department freezer and then put in a call to Chris. This had occurred two days after N-Z's release. Chris had gone over to pick up the carcass as soon as his schedule allowed. The band numbers confirmed it was the rehab peregrine. "I did not want to call you with the news until I was sure," Chris said.

"But what was he doing in the road, Chris?" I repeated.

"He had been hunting. He had a dove in his talons when he was picked up. It was still in his talons when I took him from the freezer."

"Good," I said, and I knew this was not the reply Chris expected. I could not help being pleased N-Z had successfully caught his own dinner. "He was *hunting*, Chris." If N-Z had been killed just sitting in the road, I would have worried he had been in too much pain to fly. If he had died from starvation, our decision to release N-Z would have been wrong. I wondered if he had strained his injured wing during the hunt and had not been able to escape the approaching car. This would forever remain a mystery. "N-Z was out on his own, doing what he does best. I am so sorry he was killed, but he was free and fulfilling his destiny as a hunter when it happened. I am glad I was able be part of returning him to the wild," I told Chris.

Together, Chris and I pondered how someone could have run down a sizable bird of prey on a country highway on a clear summer morning. Why didn't the driver swerve or slow down enough to keep from hitting the peregrine? Together, Chris and I mourned the passing of a rare and beautiful falcon. I had bid N-Z good-bye in the hope he would live a long life, and that he would migrate and come home to New Hampshire to mate and raise young. I had thought one day I might look skyward to see the shape of a wild peregrine and fancy it was my old friend or perhaps one of his children. Now that could never happen.

The news about N-Z left me with a sense of loss, but there was little time to mope. Summer days were shortening, and change was in the wind. I was working as much as possible with Witch, and nearly every flight was a new, hair-raising adventure. In many ways Witch was the ideal falcon. She was loyal, sweet, strong, and courageous. But her youthful high spirits were making me crazy.

At first the Overlook field was the answer to flying the youngster in a larger, safer place, but it didn't last for long. Witch's circles over the land as it dropped added many feet to her height in the air. This was great until she went into overdrive and suddenly widened her circle over the highway. The sight of her flying about three feet above the roadway terrified me, so I moved operations farther down in the field. Witch countered by widening her circles still more, which included a big white barn with a turkey pen. Then she began to spend more time flying across the highway to the turkey pen than she spent in flying back to me. I hastily nixed the Overlook field. I didn't want to envision her becoming a hood ornament for one of the local pickups, nor did I like the idea of retrieving her from the farmer's turkey coop.

Next we tried a school playing field. Witch negotiated this field at top speed, turning on her side near the trees bordering the edges like a race car using the high curves of a speedway. This field was obviously too small, so we moved on to another school field. She took to this larger field with the same scorching speed and low altitude, bobbing over fences and doing a strafing run just over the heads of the high school marching band practicing there. Her return on the lure signal, flying in and out of the goalposts, almost finished me.

The only thing left was to get over to the falconry field at the Timberdoodle Club where there were pheasants and other game birds to chase. I needed to get her away from busy roads and marching bands and onto catching prey. I loaded up my Jeep with Witch hooded and riding perched on a cadge and Injun, the Harris' hawk, in his giant hood. We were able to make the journey to Timberdoodle once or twice a week throughout the fall. At Timberdoodle there was hardly any trouble for Witch to get into.

By now Injun and I had been hunting partners for nine years. Together we had done demonstrations, talks, and lots of hunting. Hunting with a hawk is in many ways less complex than hunting with a falcon. There isn't the burning speed of the stoop or the tendency to "peregrinate," which means their propensity for wandering the skies. If the partnership with the hawk is working—meaning you have flushed game for him regularly—the hawk will stay fairly close by. He'll take a perch in a tree overhead, follow you from tree to tree as you walk a cover, and wait for you to flush the prey out for him to chase and catch. This closeness allows you to keep some measure of control (and, at best, you have only a slim margin of control at all) over any unfolding situation.

Like my dog, Injun always knew by the rattle of the Jeep when we reached the dirt road to Timberdoodle. His bells jingled as he excitedly moved from foot to foot. I would take out Injun and work over most of the field before coming back to the Jeep to put him away and then take out Witch. I tried not to hunt cock pheasant but to focus instead on chukars, Hun partridge, and quail, as Injun was not large enough to take pheasants easily. Even so, the game birds we most often encountered were big, strong cock pheasants which outweighed my Harris's. The hen pheasants were fewer in number because they were the ones most often killed and eaten by the wild hawks. These hawks were a problem for me as well as they were for the pheasants because they were not adverse to the taste of Harris's hawk or peregrine falcon.

Even without wild hawks prowling about, it was hard to get pheasants to break cover with a peregrine flying overhead, so Witch and I had a hard time catching game. The cock pheasants at Timberdoodle were veterans at avoiding flying raptors. Whenever we spotted a pheasant, it was most often running to the woods rather than taking off in flight. Even so, the introduction of game was improving Witch's flights. She was flying higher and more purposefully. I also knew I had to get Stormy working with my falcons so we could locate and flush game birds more frequently.

One day as I was taking Injun back to the Jeep after hunting, something very unusual happened. As I approached the vehicle, I could see Witch had dislodged her hood to cast it off her head. Having Witch unhooded did not pose a problem, as she was tethered to her cadge, but it did mean she was able to see the lure I held. I put Injun away into his giant hood by opening the rear passenger door. When I opened the rear lift-gate and tossed Injun's lure inside, Witch made a jump to get it and was caught up short.

Witch's jump towards the food set the next event in motion. Suddenly I was eye-to-eye with a wild juvenile peregrine circling me and the car. He barely cleared the open lift-gate of the Jeep. One circle and he took off into the sky. He must have come out of the woods and had been watching us. The pounce Witch made towards the lure instigated an instantaneous come-and-get-it reaction from the hungry young falcon. Momentarily, he had crossed the boundary nature places between the wild and mankind. I smiled at his retreating shape as he rose into the heavens. At least brazen Witch was not the only risk-taking teenaged falcon in the world.

As we all know, catastrophes are often the result of mistakes. I've made plenty of errors in my falconry career. Sometimes I have come off lightly and thanked my lucky stars. Other times, the outcome of an error comes crashing down. Then there is the heartbreak. Despite how much one may ache, one must face the choice to go on, learn, and become better, or to pack it all up and never venture out again. My way has always been to go on, but this doesn't mean I forget the pain. I do not think I am singular in this. When one becomes a falconer, one accepts that the highs are high and the lows are low.

In late October I had promised a demonstration for a teacher friend at his school, so I loaded Injun and Witch into the Jeep and headed down to Wilton. The first part of the program for the fifth-graders was my talk about falconry and Injun's flight. Everything went fine, and then I made my first mistake. After putting Injun away in his carrier, I decided to fly Witch at the large park in front of the school. I was itching to get her into the air, and I reasoned she felt the same way. The park looked big to me, but in reality it was probably no bigger than the schoolyards where we had flown in early September. It was mostly open except for a line of trees on each of three sides where the park ended at a street. Buildings surrounded the park. I unhooded Witch and stretched out my gloved arm from which she took flight. Before she had gone halfway around the circumference of the park in her signature style, fifteen feet off the ground and at supersonic speed, I knew something was very wrong with my flight plan.

I know biologists don't like to ascribe emotions to animals and birds, but I'm convinced that falcons get angry. They get bored. They go into fits of pique. The set of Witch's body and wings coupled with the fact that she didn't turn her head towards me as she circled, signaled that I was flying a bird who was angry at the boring flight pattern. I should have known better. Witch had been developing beautifully at Timberdoodle where there was open area and, above all, game birds. She took one look around and must have seen no potential for finding pheasants. She may as well have tossed her head and stomped her feet like an infuriated diva when she shot over the rooftops towards the top of the hill above us.

Then I made another mistake. In my panic, I ran after my bird. When flying falcons a falconer has to remain in the same location from where the bird flew because a trained falcon will nearly always come back to that spot. But all rational thought was discarded as I raced after my bird. Well, "raced" is a relative term. I was fifty-four, short-legged, plump, and it was all uphill. I got halfway up the hill when I stopped to catch my breath and look around at the empty sky. I blew my whistle and swung my lure. I turned and ran back, desperate to see my Witch back at her starting point. My teacher friend rushed up to me as I entered the park. "She came back. She was looking for you!" he exclaimed.

There was no sign of my bird.

"They went back behind the school. She is in the woods back there."

I had no breath to speak and move at the same time. I was in too much panic to question his choice of pronouns. "There," he pointed, and I saw my falcon sitting on a limb about fifteen feet up in a tree.

I swung my lure. Witch left her perch and headed towards me. "She brought another bird back with her," my friend said as she burst from the grove with a big shape in close pursuit. Witch passed over me. I saw her look down but she could not pause. An enormous red-tailed hawk was right behind her. My heart turned to ice. My bird was flying for her life, and there was nothing I could do to help her.

My brain foggily recorded that I was frantically running downhill through the town like a madwoman in the effort to keep my falcon in view, dodging cars as I ran, careening down twisted, paved streets, my eyes focused on the sky above. I remembered all too well the lesson learned from N-Z about a falcon not landing and making itself vulnerable. This situation was incalculably worse than the rainstorm with N-Z. Witch tried to stay near me, but every time she hovered over me the fearsome shape would come in just behind her. If she slowed, the hawk would strike at her. Witch could counter by moving and gaining height, but the red-tail had the advantage and would return to the attack position.

Being young and inexperienced, Witch had no skills to evade this killer. She had only her instincts to keep moving and rising. The red-tail, however, was a mistress of the art of pursuit, of aerial combat, and, I knew, of killing prey. Today her prey was my peregrine. As I neared the mill section of town down by the river, the two shapes hung like twin kites far, far up in the sky. I knew my falcon was both frightened and tiring. As I reached the river, it was to see the two shapes drop lower. The birds blended with the darkness of the ridgeline on the western side of the Souhegan River. That was last I saw of Witch.

I was alone, on foot, and exhausted. My car was probably no more than a mile away, but it was a steep uphill trek. Now my bird was on the other side of the river, uphill again, and across the state's major highway. I needed my vehicle to follow her. I felt like I was moving through molasses. My lungs were on fire, my heart was pounding. Just then a delivery truck headed up the street. I jumped in front of it and flagged the driver to a stop. I told him in abbreviated fashion that I was a falconer whose bird was being chased by a larger raptor, and I desperately needed to get back to my car at the schoolyard. The young man's eyes grew big. He said nothing but motioned for me to take the seat beside him. I climbed aboard and sat on the edge of the seat to steady myself as the truck negotiated the steep incline to the school. It took only a few minutes to reach my Jeep. The ride had given me a chance to recover enough breath to thank him.

By the time I returned to the mill yard, the red-tail was sunning herself on a branch hanging over the far side of the river. She looked well-fed. My heart clenched painfully. She would never have pulled out of a pursuit she was so clearly winning. I knew she had killed and eaten my young falcon. As I watched, she lazily left her perch and began her flight back to the orchard on the hilltop. I was tired, too discouraged for tears, and sick inside, but I combed the mill yard area and then drove the roads of the western ridgeline. School buses passed by me with homebound students. Now it was late afternoon and the sun was low, leaving the river and mills in shadow. Reluctantly, knowing Jim would be troubled if I was not back soon, I turned the Jeep in the direction of home.

Once there, I told Jim about the events leading up to Witch's loss. He was as sad as I was and also believed that she was truly gone, something I accepted even as I knew I had to do all I could to find her on the slim chance she had survived. So, I was up before dawn the next morning driving towards Wilton, equipped with quail and my whistle and lure.

Overnight a front had blown through, and it no longer felt like fall. Raindrops were interspersed with pellets of sleet. The keen edge of winter was on the wind. At times I drove through snow squalls that obliterated my sight and forced me to slow the car to a crawl. I covered every roadway west, east, south, and north. During the next week, I walked over riverbanks and through forests, over cultivated fields and hayfields. I wended my way through industrial parks and hazardous waste dump areas. The sun did not shine. It grew colder. I caught a cold and spent the days coughing as I walked. The cord of the lure wore blisters on my fingers and hand. These broke and bled, and still I hunted, heartbroken and searching for the sight of a glad, gay young peregrine eager to join me and return home.

The word that my falcon had gone missing spread like wildfire throughout Wilton. For many days the phone rang with sightings and suggestions. Sometimes the callers just wanted to know if my beautiful bird had found her way home. I followed every lead, knowing it was highly unlikely it had been my bird. The callers were trying to be helpful, so I listened and responded. My falcon had been seen in a tree in a field in Antrim. The caller was certain it was my bird because, after all, it was big and black . . . just like a falcon. At the same time my bird was seen in Antrim, she was also allegedly chasing birds from a bird feeder in Wilton. It had to be my bird, the caller explained, because . . . And what would follow would be both an earnest and improbable description. I responded politely to these people. I went to each location reported. I was out searching from sunup to sundown for five days.

I saw the hilltop red-tail on several of those days and also innumerable raptors inhabiting the valley following the river south. The raptors seemed to wind up at the fields in Milford. Undoubtedly the state fish hatchery nearby was the reason. It had many coin-operated fish-food dispensers that meted out mealy pellets so visitors could feed the trout. The rodent population drawn by the dispensers must have made the area an ideal feeding spot for hawks and owls. I was astounded by the number and the variety of raptors.

At one point, I crossed the highway to an industrial area. There I met a pint-size red-tailed hawk who never ventured from the telephone poles over the weed-covered ditch between the road and the railroad tracks. He was so small he could not have managed to take much in the way of prey, and he followed me as I swung the lure. I threw it down between us, curious to see what he would do. He nearly came for it, but restrained himself at the last moment. I was sorry to see him so hungry and realized he likely had subsisted all summer on the frogs in the ditch water. Now that the amphibians were gone, he probably wouldn't survive the winter. I left him a bit of quail by the ditch. I bore no ill will towards red-tailed hawks—not towards this little fellow or the big red-tailed hen of the hilltop. Survival is not a given. Only those that are skilled and strong manage to do so.

When Jim and I discussed the loss of Witch, we sought some other conclusion than that she had been killed by another bird of prey. Every evening I would recount to myself the things I had done wrong or could have done better. A totally wrong choice of flight area headed the list, followed by leaving the area in panic. I have asked myself a thousand times if I had been there when she first came back, could I have retrieved her? The question will haunt me for the rest of my life. I also could have outfitted Witch with radio telemetry, which is a common practice among falconers. Telemetry would not have protected her from the red-tail, but I might have been able to track her remains during my searches. There was no guarantee this would have worked, as telemetry is notoriously unhelpful in the wooded, hilly terrain of this region.

When I spoke about it with other falconers, they were quick to remind me that the most common way trained falconry birds are lost is by being killed by wild birds of prey. This can happen when our birds are hunting and are not expecting to come under aerial attack. Wild raptors are wily about taking advantage of a vulnerable moment. Only the most experienced falconry raptors learn to beware their wild brethren. My fellow falconers were profuse in offering sympathy and kindness. They advised me not to hold myself responsible for Witch's death. One of my closest friends entreated me, "Nancy, please don't get any more falcons. It hurts you so when they die."

CHAPTER 23

Only Optimists Need Apply

There had been joy in the education I had been given by N-Z and Witch, and the lessons have stayed fresh in my mind. In the intervening years I have thought about N-Z's demise on the road. At first I blamed the fact he could not have been put up for a year of rest and resented that the regulations did not allow this. I had wondered if his death was related to lack of strength in his injured wing. But having handled more falcons and gained more experience since then, I have come to the conclusion that N-Z's own steadiness and stalwartness on his kill was what really contributed to his death. His firm stance on game was likely the factor that brought him to rehab in the first place.

There are opposing views about wildlife rehabilitation. The prevailing view of the public, and of many people who deal with wildlife conservation, is that rehabilitation reverses the damage caused by contact with human civilization. But the fact of the matter is that raptors are governed by instinct, and rehabbed raptors will return to the same successful hunting areas where they were injured, no matter how dangerous. And very often the second time is terminal.

Life in the wild is not a kind, gentle existence. It is hunt or be hunted. The strong, the skilled, and the lucky do not enter rehab. Law dictates that releasable creatures will be returned to the wild. In the past this was thought to be beneficial to wild populations. Eventually wildlife and conservation agencies banded together to do an exhaustive study on the effect of rehabilitating injured wildlife for release. The statistics were very plain, especially regarding birds of prey: A raptor taken into rehabilitation results in one less raptor in the wild. Returned to the wild, this same raptor does not increase the wild population by one, but instead becomes a "zero cipher." In other words, once taken out becomes forever taken out.

Because of the precipitously dangerous lives lived by predators, the decks are stacked against successful rehab and release. Preparing a young, orphaned raptor for life in the wild is difficult, as a rehabber must replicate the ways parent birds instill skills in the young. In the case of injured raptors, it is assumed the bird will repeat whatever risky business got him into trouble, so recuperation and restoration to the wild do not ensure living happily ever after. In addition to the grim statistics, the conclusion of the agencies' comprehensive survey was that rehabilitation of wildlife was a way to satisfy the public's view that an injured creature must be "saved," a natural response from a culture taught to treasure the environment and nature, but not of great consequence in terms of maintaining wild populations.

For some, standing at the sidelines and not participating in rehabilitation efforts is not an option. They cannot help themselves; they step forward and get involved despite the grim outlook of the statistics, despite the difficulties, laws, and licensing fees with which one must comply to take up rehabilitation work. Licensed rehabilitators are amazingly dedicated individuals. These optimistic people have struggled through the permitting process and jump to rescue, to heal, and to raise the young. Knowing full well the statistics, they convince themselves *this* time it will be different. *This* will be the one that doesn't become the zero cipher. Sometimes the rehabilitator is right. Even sometimes is enough for those who do wildlife rehab.

PART THREE

A LIFE FILLED WITH RAPTORS

CHAPTER 24

Bubba

The year wound down to end, and as it did the passage of time softened my sadness. Injun filled the void left by the loss of Witch to a degree, but I missed the magical feeling of working with a peregrine. There was the financial loss as well. N-Z had required a huge amount of time and work, not to mention the food and equipment outlay required for rehabbing a bird. Witch had set me back for well over a thousand dollars. I would have to save for a long time to be able to afford another like her. I had to ask myself, considering the money invested, the work, and all the pain, would I do it again? Would I jump wholeheartedly into another year of raising a bird I risked losing whenever I set her free to fly, or of helping another invalid regain his wings no matter what odds faced him? I know the answer now just as I knew the answer then. The expenses were more than repaid in full by sharing my life with peregrines.

Bubba was not young when he came to us. Vic, a falcon breeder Jim and I knew, called to ask if I would accept the "loan" of a peregrine. (Loan was Vic's way of saying gift, with a "string attached".) Vic had "loaned" me the beautiful but barren female peregrine falcon, Lass. Now he was offering a male. The bird was presently in a northeastern state with another breeder named Ed whose mews were overcrowded. The breeder was having no breeding success with this bird. I explained I could not take another bird, but my husband could. I thought Jim might wish to add this tiercel to his falconry permit, as master falconers were allowed three birds at a time on their license. Vic proceeded in barroom-bawdy language to tell me what had precipitated him to "loan" the falcon to the northeastern breeder.

Vic had been wearing a special hat that falcon breeders use to collect sperm from the male falcon in order to artificially inseminate a female. In this procedure, the imprinted falcon usually accepts the breeder as its mate and will light upon the hat to copulate with it while it is on the breeder's head. The semen filters through many holes of the outer covering and is then collected in the upturned brim. Vic's feisty male bird would have nothing to do with the hat. Worse yet, he seemed more bent on attacking than on lovemaking, and the portion of Vic's anatomy to which he had affixed his talons involved Vic's rear. The incident was the reason Vic had given up working with the tiercel. His description made me wince as I listened.

So this is why we found ourselves driving to the rural countryside of upstate New York on a mission to collect a peregrine with a horrid reputation for intractableness. Ed, who had the bird at the time, was both a respected breeder and a knowledgeable falconer with whom we had long been acquainted. Upon our arrival he greeted us warmly and showed us around his breeding facility before he went into the mew to catch the peregrine. The bird fought Ed like a tiger. Angry shrieking from the agitated tiercel made us wonder what was in store for us when we reached home. Exiting the mew, Ed relayed some of the details he knew about Jim's new bird.

The falcon was a Santa Cruz Predatory Bird Research Facility imprint of Peale's peregrine extraction (Peale's are a strain of peregrines native to the Pacific Northwest and noted for their large size) intended to be part of a peregrine breeding project, but no breeder had achieved success with it. Imprinting is the preferred method of producing birds planned for breeding programs and also for producing docile and calm falcons for falconry. However, imprinting that has gone wrong in any aspect can create a terrifyingly aggressive creature that cannot be easily handled. Knowing the reputation of the Santa Cruz program, it was a given the bird would have been raised correctly. What had happened in the meantime to create a peregrine with such a personality disorder?

Physically, this fellow had a malformed stub of a talon, which was evidence of a past injury. Was this a clue to what had caused him to have such negative reactions about being handled? An imprinted bird loaded with Peale's genes would normally be an asset to peregrine propagation. Because this fellow's habit was to attack the breeder instead of landing on the special hat to copulate, he had "flunked out" of the breeding program. Nonbreeding, imprinted peregrines from breeding operations are commonly returned to falconry, so what Jim planned to do with the tiercel was a very good solution.

Our worries about what faced us when we reached home came to nothing. The fellow had calmed down during the trip. We learned, however, not to expect consistency. This classically beautiful falcon was vociferous and volatile one minute, nonchalantly relaxed the next. He reminded me of the boys I had known as schoolmates when growing up in the South: easy-going outdoorsmen and hunters, but quick to act if something riled their sensitivities. I remarked he was a "bubba." The word fitted him to a T. If peregrines drove pickups, this bird would have had a red one with lights on top, an air horn, and chrome running boards. Ever after, he was known to us as "Bubba."

Jim soon found he had a uniquely talented peregrine. Bubba seemed to enjoy being at the forefront whenever we did falconry demonstrations, conservation programs, or school presentations. He was the consummate showman. Never mind that he shrieked bloody murder when Jim would hood him to take him home. On stage he was the quintessential peregrine falcon to thousands of adoring fans. Whether it was an Audubon program or part of Discover Wild New Hampshire Day, Bubba would carry on his own personal brand of entertainment. With his rolling, bowlegged swagger, he would get as close to the audience as his leash allowed. The crowd would settle down to sit cross-legged and stare back. They were mesmerized. This short-circuited, temperamental falcon would settle himself on his tummy in the grass and commune like a guru with his horde of followers.

Eventually Bubba decided Jim was his person, although Jim's job had become one requiring frequent travel. Consequently much of the bird care fell to me. Despite this, to Bubba's way of thinking, I was relegated to "invader" status while Jim was adored. When Jim was around, Bubba would race to his mew window to call entreaties to my husband. Jim could enter the mew, and Bubba would quietly allow himself to be jessed and leashed. As soon as Jim stepped with him out of the mew, however, a rodeo would ensue. After the hissy fit, Bubba would become a gentleman once again. He and I came to terms once he decided that whenever I came to his mew, it was to take him along on a school trip. Bubba liked to settle as close to the youngsters as possible and watch them as avidly as they watched him.

Because he was imprinted on humans, he responded to me as though I were another falcon. Peregrines bow when another peregrine flies onto their ledge. Whether it is a greeting, an assertion of the peregrine's territory, or has some other meaning in peregrine speak, I do not know. As I faced him Bubba would bow to me with dignity. His behavior both educated and delighted the children.

Bubba became an important and very vocal member of our family. Greeting Jim with calls whenever my husband stepped out of the house was only one part of his repertoire. The old tiercel surveyed everyone who entered our driveway. It was as though he felt it his duty to keep watch and notify us of dangers. He seemed to hate the men who came to mow our fields and lawns in particular. As soon as Bubba spied their telltale orange T-shirts, he would begin screaming the peregrine war cry. Because he enjoyed watching humans, we frequently kept him perched and tethered in our front hallway. Both of our grandchildren learned to check if Bubba was perched there before they proceeded on the way upstairs.

We had lived with him for eight years when one autumn Bubba began having a hard time flying up to get his meal on his shelf. It was a sign the falcon was aging. We knew Bubba would not last the winter. Falcons and hawks do not decline into old age, but when they exhibit certain indications, we know their lives are close to ending. Nursing and special care are to no avail. The life force of raptors is a fierce, bright flame extinguishing itself into nothingness like magic. We have learned to accept this as stoically as the birds.

Soon after we noticed Bubba's decline, Jim had to leave on a weeklong business trip. Before he left, he took a moment to call me at work. Jim liked to look in on each of our birds before leaving for a trip. "I checked the birds," he said, "and Bubba is on the floor of his mew. His wings twitched when I spoke to him, but he could not rise. I think he will surely be gone by the time you get home." There was a tinge of sadness in his voice. He knew his old friend was not going to be there to greet him when he returned.

I hate discovering one of our birds has died, even when it is expected. Jim had found his falcon in the death throes. Knowing the old raptor would die within moments, it was kindest to leave him where he felt safest. When I got home after work, I immediately went to check on Bubba. I found his body nestled on the floor.

There is a sentiment among falconers that prevents the public show of emotion over a raptor death. A display of grief would be contrary to the very nature of nature, and I think most falconers share that belief. We are sad when a friend such as Bubba passes on, but raptors live and die like they fly—they are here and then they are gone in a flash. When death comes suddenly and unexpectedly, we hurt, sometimes badly. Our feelings are raw, but falconers most often keep it private. We face the world with the declaration that, whether a falconry bird or a bird here for rehab, each has left us with the gift of increased experience and indelible memories.

CHAPTER 25

Contract Attorneys and Partnerships

The falconry partnership gives me the opportunity to prove myself worthy to my bird, and gives the bird what she exists on Earth for in the first place—hunting and catching game. Each partner derives a benefit from the partnership. The benefit spilling over to me is my bird and I continue, day after day, working together. This means doing many other activities with my bird besides hunting. I may fly my bird to condition her or to build up her stamina and speed. I may fly her to demonstrate falconry to educate an audience. My hawks often are scheduled to take part in classes at our falconry school, where they will be flying to and from students. In between, I must get my birds out and into the hunting field.

By renewing the hunting partnership with my birds, I can continue non-hunting activities with my hawks. If they were not regularly hunted, our raptors would become discouraged. My strong partnership with them would begin to erode. They would depend less upon me to fulfill my role as a disturbance to scare up game. They would begin ranging farther and farther from me when I flew them. They would cease flying to students that they saw only for one class. I do not want this to happen with my birds. Each is to me an individual I prize beyond monetary worth. My plan to keep my birds working with me throughout their lives requires a great deal of time and effort expended in their favorite activity—hunting.

When I became a licensed falconer, I didn't always know where our life with raptors would lead. Our contact with people curious about falconry grew so much that the best way to manage the demand for information became the establishment of a falconry school. Having a place where non-falconers could learn about hawks and falcons has led to some unexpected and treasured lessons—for me as well as for my students. Because of the school, we have come into possession of a number of Harris' hawks. I have, consequently, been taught a lot I did not know about these hawks beyond the partnership they share with me. To say I was surprised one day at finding my Harris's had instituted their own system of contracts with my students is an understatement.

I was explaining to my students about how the partnership with a hawk is developed and maintained. "I never blow the whistle without having food ready for the hawk, or without having the lure garnished with food for the falcon. I may thump upon my glove with my ungloved hand, or give a chirp with my lips. I do this to call my hawk to my hand from his perch or to summon him closer during a hunt. He does not expect to find food waiting for him at the thump on the glove. My bird realizes these signals are different than the whistle to return to me. If the whistle had sounded, I would have had food on the glove. Because the falcon on high is beyond earshot of the whistle, the same is true of the lure. It always carries a tidbit when I swing it."

This is how I read the body language of the hawk, I told them. "I know my hawk is responsive to me when he lands and turns to face me. If I don't see that behavior, I know I have a bird who is not responsive. One reason for this might be I have misjudged his flying weight and released him when he was actually overweight. Then, I call him down." I made it plain to the students that the bird doesn't return to the glove to collect a reward for good behavior, but comes instead because I am the "safe place" he trusts, and I present an easy opportunity for food. The raptor at flying weight will therefore return to me to collect the tidbit he sees as already being his. His instinct prompts him to do so. When we are in the field, a call to the glove holds little draw for a hawk eager to maintain a high position for watching the action, so I switch to calling him in with the lure. Our strong hunting partnership is what makes it all work. I had never given a thought as to what the hawks expected from my students until that day.

After my preliminary instruction, we started flying the hawk. After one of the gentlemen had had the hawk fly to him several times, he extended his gloved hand and said, "I bet he will come for no food at all." The male Harris's flying that day was Scout, and he was swift. My exclamation to the student to drop his hand before my bird landed came too late. Scout paused just a split second, looked down at the glove empty of the tidbit he had been expecting, and in a flash took wing again up to the barn roof.

"You should not have done that," I admonished. "You broke the contract. I doubt this bird will come back to you."

My Harris's hawks know that when we are standing about with a group of students, we are not on a hunt. Prior to this moment, I had not given this much thought. I assumed my hawks would fly to my students because I ensured that my hawks hunted often enough to maintain their partnership with *me*. I was wrong. The Harris's hawks already had everything scoped out. When I think I know it all, they show me something new.

When the man made his move and Scout reacted to it, it occurred to me that perhaps my hawks had a second contract that only applied to students. My students were not hunting partners; therefore, the "contract" with them meant that they darn well better have a tidbit ready on the glove whenever they extend an arm. Suddenly I knew what Scout's reaction would be before he completed the flight to the barn roof. He landed and then, sure enough, turned his back to the offending student. He afterwards returned to the three other students on their turns, but shunned the man who had broken the "gentleman's agreement."

I should have expected this. In the wild, Harris's hawks have a complex social order that requires working in multiple relationships. It is very easy for the falconer with his hawk to practice something routine and never intend for the motion to become imbedded in the raptor's consciousness. How the raptor reads and responds to our unconscious but repeated physical actions is often a surprise to the falconer. Sometimes the unexpected cue can be nothing more than a sound. When I started out with Injun, I had a tidbit case with a Velcro closure. One evening at a conservation presentation, a young girl at the back of the audience was using a notebook known as a trapper-keeper. Each time the girl opened the notebook, the scratchy sound of Velcro opening was heard. Each time Injun became sharp set, expecting a food opportunity.

Having strangers in the flight area has become a new signal to my hawks here at the school. A new situation has been set up, and they have risen to the occasion. They, in effect, whip out that "contract" about students *always* having food on an extended glove. The hunting drive of these keen predators must be satisfied on a regular basis (by me), but obviously Harris's are able to concoct, with more complexity than I had expected, new partnerships. Clearly, not only do my Harris's hawks understand terms of agreement as well as or better than a successful attorney, they also write additional contracts to fit new situations that arise.

CHAPTER 26

Summer Flights

Flying for exhibitions and classes in the spring and summer was not something I was used to doing as a falconer because falconers put birds up for the molt through the summer. Flying after the molt is done starts in late summer to prepare birds for the fall and winter hunting season. There are difficulties flying in spring and summer that one doesn't face later in the year.

One year, long before I began the falconry school, I was asked by the local Cub Scout pack to speak at the last meeting for the year in June. I did not want to disappoint the kids, and Injun had finished his molt quite early, so I agreed to have the pack meet at our home. When they assembled in my yard, I gave a short talk to the Cubs and then turned Injun loose. He took a perch in one of the spruce trees over the drive and chanced upon a nest full of baby robins. Needless to say, this did not work out well for the robin family. Injun, of course, was pleased with his discovery. He flew a great demonstration for the Cub pack despite being harassed by a pair of furious parent robins and having already had a meal of robin nestlings. Later in the fall, and for years after, when I flew him at home, he always stopped by the nest, now empty, just to see if another tasty surprise awaited him.

On another occasion we were hired to do a summer program for the Fort at Number 4, a re-creation of an eighteenth-century fort sited on the banks of the Connecticut River in Charlestown, New Hampshire. We were familiar with the fort, but when we arrived, I looked at the surroundings like a raptor would instead of a tourist. There was plenty to interest a raptor, and none of it had a thing to do with life in the old days. We received a few scoldings from birds with nests located in a copse of trees nearby. I scouted the area, trying to establish the safest, most viewable location for the flight. It seemed best to avoid the nest-bearing trees.

The Fort at Number 4 is a large square of palisades, with an interior square bounded by living quarters and gates at two ends. There were lookout towers, too. All of the buildings were constructed of hewn logs. The interior square would make a good area for a flight demonstration, I thought. It had an unobstructed viewing area and lots of perching places, and we were out of sight of those pesky bird nests. Little did I suspect an adventure was about to begin.

It was Jazz's first spring with me. She was a Harris's hawk without much hunting experience, but she was working well on the lure. I was confident she would accomplish a good flight demonstration. I stood in the center of the fort and cast her off. Out from holes, nooks, and crannies in the logs and palisade walls erupted hundreds of swallows hell-bent on driving my hawk from the vicinity. The swallow army formed into a large, dark cloud flying hot on the heels of my inexperienced hawk as she sought to out-fly it. I was afraid that in her panic she might crash into one of the structures or fly up and over the palisades to be chased to goodness knows where—across the river, over the highway, or to any number of places from which I would have trouble retrieving her.

Visitors to the fort watched in awe as the spectacle took place. My hawk was flying as fast as she could around the inside of the fort walls with the murderous black cloud right behind her. Sometimes one of the smaller birds would dart forward to take a whack at her. Jazz could not be distracted from her escape flight to cast a glance at the glove I held out to retrieve her.

Suddenly something wondrous happened. Jazz spread her wings and put on the brakes in midair. Caught by surprise, the cloud of swallows separated around her and re-formed without losing speed. Jazz pumped her wings and started flying right after them. Now a different sort of race was on! Scores of the swallows darted off to safety into their nest holes. The cloud was diminishing as Jazz chased it. Eventually Jazz was pursuing only a handful of swallows, which, with a flick of their wings, dashed out of sight between the logs and under the eaves. I hastily pulled the lure out of my game pocket and swung it for Jazz, who turned at the sound of my whistle and caught it handily.

There was a round of applause from the onlookers. They had been treated to a far more exciting display than I had intended, and they had no idea how relieved I was things had worked out. For Jazz, of course, it was an important learning experience and contributed to what made her such a fine hunter for the rest of her life. For me, it was a lesson, too, on the unexpected difficulties presented by flying raptors during the summer months when songbirds and other small birds are busy building nests, raising young, flying about everywhere, and militantly defending their territories.

One spring morning, a class turned into a stellar moment for my Harris's hawk named Smoke. I had assembled my students in the backyard for the flight portion of the class. Smoke was brought out, weighed, and proved to be exactly at her flying weight, a bit above thirty-two ounces. I cast her off to take a perch on a limb overhead.

I was busy explaining to the students how the next few moments would proceed and failed to notice Smoke's attention was riveted on a large rock around which we had recently planted three small ornamental shrubs. Suddenly she dropped from the tree to seize a mole popping up from the base of one of the shrubs. I hurried over to find something that resembled a fat, furry gray kielbasa in her talons. No wonder the new shrubs had not been doing well. As fast as lightning, her other foot struck down into the mole tunnel and came up with another fat, furry kielbasa-mole! On behalf of the shrubs, I was thrilled. But this didn't bode well for flying her for the class.

When a raptor has caught, killed, and eaten quarry, the bird is ready to find a nice, comfortable perch upon which to sit, relax, and digest. Our agenda at the moment was flying, the direct opposite of what would transpire if nature took its course. I dropped to my knees beside my bird, now clutching her "two-for-the-price-of-one" quarry, and offered her a chick. Smoke dropped her moles to hop to my glove, the moles were swiftly deposited out of sight into my pocket, and class resumed. After class, I put her away in her mew with her two prizes. I knew she would not fly for days after consuming them, but she certainly had earned them. Now whenever I cast Smoke off, she takes a perch on the same limb to check out those bushes. Like the lucky fisherman with a favorite fishing hole, this must be her "sweet spot."

Because of a class schedule that starts our falconry school in mid-April, I need to have birds done molting and ready to be taken down to flying weight. In the confines of our well-lit basement, the Harris's begin and end their molts due to the artificial "daylight." I work birds into the class schedule once their molts are done.

One summer when there was lots of wild bird activity in my yard, the tables were turned on Scout. I sent him aloft during a class and when he did not return from the barn roof, I looked up to find out why. I saw Scout sitting, practically back on his tail, as an angry hummingbird buzzed to and fro inches from his face. When I called Scout away, he looked happy to come down from the area of confrontation. He had no desire to tangle with the angry little male who, ounce for ounce, clearly outdid him on the aggression scale. A tiny hummingbird "reading the riot act" to a hawk was enough to keep my class of students chuckling for quite a while.

CHAPTER 27

Moving Day for Falcons

When it comes to understanding the behavior of hawks and falcons, my husband is often more intuitive than I am. I need to see a situation unfold in order for the tumblers to fall into place in my brain. Frequently Jim and I reach the same conclusion. The following story illustrates how an out-of-the-ordinary situation enhanced my understanding of peregrines late one spring.

It began with an invitation from Chris Martin, the Audubon peregrine biologist, to help move three hatchling peregrines from a dangerous, narrow window ledge on the ninth floor of a building in Manchester, the largest city in New Hampshire. The plan was to recover the young eyasses from the ledge and take them to a nest box Chris had installed on the roof of the same building. We were eager to join him in this adventure, knowing that whatever transpired would be another learning experience. Admittedly, part of our quick acceptance of his invitation was the thrill of dealing once again with wild peregrines.

On the appointed morning, we met Chris at the building where the peregrines had nested. We wondered why Chris felt the youngsters were in danger at the site the female had chosen. We soon found out why.

When we got to the ninth floor, we seemed to attract people from every hallway on our progression to the window ledge. By the time we reached it, we had been joined by a group who had for the last weeks been taking personal interest in the welfare of the infant peregrines. It was like a gathering of fond uncles, aunties, and godparents at a christening. Most of them had their cameras with them.

As soon as I spied the window, I understood Chris's concern. The window ledge was just that—a narrow ledge running across a solid windowpane. At the outer edge of the ledge was a concrete balustrade standing about two feet high. The space between each of the concrete spindles was no wider than four inches. The distance between the window and the balustrade was no more than five or six inches. It was incredibly cramped. *What was she* thinking?! I wondered.

The female had been observed landing on the top of the balustrade and then dropping down into the space on the ledge. The male, being smaller, was able to sail in for a landing between the spindles. To exit, both adults squeezed through the spindles to eject their bodies into freefalls. There was absolutely no place for a youngster to stand to work its wings. There was no space from which to fledge. With the three young all at the fuzzy stage, there was barely enough space for the family. Once they began sprouting primary and tail feathers, there wouldn't be enough room for the three to live, let alone for the parents to join them when they flew in with food.

Chris maneuvered the windows above the ledge, opening them slightly so that he could stick his shoulder and arm out. He then lowered what looked like a triangular butterfly net down to scoop up one baby falcon at a time while the narrowness of the window opening protected him from the onslaught of the angry parents.

Baby falcons are so homely as to be cute. A youngster caught up in the net and pressed against the window gave the arresting vision of "peregrine under glass." All the young had obviously been eating well. With big beady eyes peering through the pane at all of us and exposed pink tummies showing through their down, each was carefully lifted upward one at a time. Chris was focused on the task at hand, ignoring the din produced by two very vocal parent birds. Every once in a while a taloned foot would slash through the window opening as one of the parents dove past, but he managed to remain unscathed. Finally all three babies had been brought into the room. Chris began banding each with our assistance.

Outside, the adults were diving back and forth, raising a terrific hue and cry. In downtown Manchester on a lovely spring day, it was impossible for the racket to go unnoticed. Looking down, I saw a group of people gathered watching and pointing at our window. Across the street, up and down the building that faced us, the windows were full of people who worked in those offices. Afterward, there was quite a public reaction to "moving day." Some enjoyed the show. Some felt concern turn to relief when they realized the disturbance was so the young falcons could be moved to a safer place. Some were perturbed there had been any interference at all with the peregrines. Most of the onlookers did not realize the entire process was being carried out with approval from federal and state wildlife agencies and was performed by a professional biologist from the Audubon Society.

After the banding, the young were loaded into a pet carrier, and we headed up to the roof. Jim and I waited while Chris negotiated the uneven rooftop to leave the young peregrines at the nest box. When he rejoined us, we headed over to a building across the street where a spotting scope had been focused on the nest box. We admitted to each other that we were tense about moving the falcons from one spot to another. Would the parents accept the new location to take up the care of their offspring?

Once settled at the spotting scope, we watched the agitated peregrine adults as they returned again and again to the window ledge nest site. The female perched and looked down into the empty space on the ledge. The male flew through the narrow spaces in the balustrade and then turned to fly back out. Employees of the nest site building came to the window to see what was going on, and the adults dove at them. The peregrines flew to the building from which we watched. They took perches on the cornices at either end and they watched, too. Then they flew back and forth over the corridor between the two facing buildings. It was a strange sensation to be above them, looking down at the tops of their wings and their backs as the pair flew below us over the busy street. We continued to watch, and we worried.

Two hours went by. It might have helped if the youngsters had gotten hungry and begun to call for food. Then perhaps the parents would hear them and find them on the roof. But these kids were exceedingly well fed. Through the scope we watched the young peregrines waddle about and then snuggle down for naps. We were beginning to question ourselves. Had we done the right thing? Would this move work out, or would we have to reverse the entire process and place the eyass falcons back into the original nest site, horridly unsuitable as it was?

The adults continued to return to the window ledge, then sail back and forth over the street. As I watched, something finally tugged at my brain. On all the flights up and down the street, to and from the window ledge, the adults were looking down. "Chris," I said, "babies don't fall *up*. The parents are looking *down* for them."

Jim agreed. "They never saw the youngsters go up onto the roof. They just saw them disappear through the window. The adults will keep looking for them there."

"I think I need to go back up on the roof," Chris said. "Maybe I can get the adults to look up and see the young birds." We enthusiastically endorsed Chris's plan.

Chris returned to the nest site building, traveled up in the elevator, and laboriously made his way to the nest box to take one of the youngsters in his hands and hold it high. This was a nice touch but hardly necessary, for as soon as he gained the roof, the adults spotted him and began to circle above him, screaming as they wheeled through the air. They might not have known where their babies had gone, but they certainly recognized the bearded baby-snatcher when they saw him again! One of them was in a full-on stoop at Chris's head when he raised the baby in his hands. The adult pulled up instead of whacking him. Chris returned the eyass to the box and left the roof as quickly as he could.

"Do you think they saw their youngsters?" Chris asked when he rejoined us. He was laughing because there was no doubt they had. But the adults had not yet joined their young on the roof, so Chris settled down to wait. He would not leave his post until he knew all was well and that the adults would accept the new site to resume caring for their young. Having witnessed the adult birds' reaction to Chris's appearance on the roof, we were more confident and elected to head for home. Once out of the building, we looked up. The adults were back on the cornices across the street from the nest box, but they were now looking up at the roof. Forty minutes later as we neared home, my cell phone rang. It was Chris. "The parents flew to the roof and landed by the nest box. They are feeding the young right now."

The peregrine family proceeded to raise the young in fairly normal fashion after the change in locale. We got frequent e-mails from the peregrine watchers in the buildings and were treated to reports as each of the three babies fledged and when they began hunting. I enjoyed the photos and the reports, but one thing still bothered me: Where would Mrs. Peregrine choose her nest site next spring?

CHAPTER 28

Cowan's Falcon "Nursery"

Prior to the relocation of Manchester's peregrine brood, we had young falcons of our own. Jim was raising Hobie, an imprinted female black gyrfalcon. About the time she outgrew her box, I received a call from a woman from a wildlife center. "Nancy," she said, "I have a little merlin here, blown from his nest when the tree was demolished in a storm, that needs to be raised. I think you are the most qualified to bring him up. Do you want to do it?" Oh, did I *ever*!

So, suddenly we were raising two young falcons. Gyrfalcons are the largest of falcons, and merlins are one of the smallest. By the time they got old enough to wear anklets and to sit on perches, we had a big, black four-pounder at one end of the hallway and a teensy mini-peregrine weighing barely five ounces at the other. The size difference illustrates the remarkable variations of the family Falconidae. One baby started out in a big air-conditioner box, while the other arrived in a carton the size of a shoebox.

Until he could be perched, the little merlin, who we named Swifty, lived in a box for sleeping and eating. As often as I could manage, he got regular periods of running around. It became easier to turn him loose in my kitchen because I could shut the doors to keep him corralled. Falcons can never be housebroken. Fortunately the oak floors cleaned up easily from the occasional drop of hawkchalk. I had to open the doors carefully whenever I entered the kitchen with Swifty on the loose. He was so tiny I was afraid I might accidentally step on him or knock him over with the door. Usually I had to look for him in hidden spots under the deacon's bench or in the corner by the dishwasher. He was the intrepid conqueror of the wilds of the kitchen!

Swifty's developing feathers were beginning to poke through his white fluff. As the feathers grew, the fluff began to shed. One day I found the youngster sopping wet. He had not yet fledged, so I was at a loss as to how he had made up to the sink. When I rounded the stove, the mystery became clear. The dogs' water dish was not quite as full as it had been, and the floor around it was covered with splashes. To Swifty, the water dish made a superb bathtub.

Before an eyass arrives at our home, a search goes on throughout the house and attic to find a suitable box. When Jim got his first gyrfalcon, the best box for the purpose (because it was the largest we had) was a vacuum cleaner box. Typical of the personality of gyr imprints, the youngster was sociable and curious. Once his legs got strong enough for him to stand and to run around, he became dissatisfied at being returned to his box at the end of his play periods or when it was nighttime. He hopped and tried to get leverage on the top of the box wall with his beak. The thuds of his landings and the scratching of his talons as he attempted his escape went on for quite a while.

In the meantime, Jim was seeking the perfect name for this bird with whom he had become totally enamored. Just when I had gotten used to calling the gyrkin (the proper term for a male gyr) one name, Jim started calling him another. I was getting tired of the scratching, and the thumping, and the name changing. "If you don't hurry up and get the bird out of that vacuum cleaner box," I threatened, "I am going to start calling him 'Hoover'!" And that's how Hoover got his name.

Once they're old enough to jump up and down, we perch young birds in the long center hallway of our house. There are doors to the outside at each end, which we open during the summer months to let in light and air. The view of the outdoors and the activity around our home are of great interest to the youngsters perched just inside the screen doors. Prior to graduating to perches, eyasses live in their boxes. Jim's habit is to keep the box right by his bedside, where he can reach down and touch the youngster or speak to it as soon as he awakes in the morning. Jim's female black gyrfalcon, Hobie, started life in a big box by our bed. Jim was in no rush to move his young falcon out of the box because he loved waking with the bird right beside him. Often he would scoop the youngster up for some side-by-side snoozing. More than once I found Hobie cuddled on the pillow next to his face, both of them dozing away.

Unlike Hoover, Jim picked Hobie's name with relative swiftness. She had been raised by a breeder in South Dakota. Jan, the falcon breeder's wife, was in charge of hand-raising the imprinted baby falcons from the time they hatched until they were shipped to their new homes. Jan does this process on her dining room table (this reassured me that Jim and I were not the singularly oddest couple in the United States). She also made it her business to know every detail of the trip, including, I think, the names of every person who would be involved in moving the falcon on and off the planes. The fortunate part is airline personnel are acutely conscious of their responsibility, but even so, much can happen on a cross-country flight.

When we were expecting Jim's new baby gyrfalcon, we got a call from the airline. "Mrs. Cowan, we have your falcon here in Minneapolis. The flight was diverted because of weather and the connection in Cleveland was missed. The bird seems fine and we will get it started on the way tomorrow as soon as possible." I called Jan to give her the news.

"Minneapolis?! What is she doing in Minneapolis?" Jan erupted.

"I have her name and number, Jan, if you need to contact her," I tried to assuage her.

"I am calling her right now, Nancy. We will have Jim's gyr sent back here directly. I am taking no chances with someone arranging a connector who does not understand how this bird must travel."

A couple of days later, Jan called with the new flight plans. "Jim is already calling this one 'The Hobo' because of all her traveling," I told Jan.

Jan started chuckling. "Several years ago," she said, "we sent a young falcon out and its flight also got complicated by bad weather. It was an older bird than your eyass, and with those we put a whole dead quail into their carriers instead of the dish of chopped quail we give younger gyrs. Even though the falcons leave here very well fed, the food is an extra bit of insurance. The older youngsters are able to tear the quail up to eat if something delays a flight and they get hungry. We got a call from the airline telling us the bird had been off-loaded from the plane until flights resumed when the weather cleared. I asked the girl who called if the falcon was okay. There was silence, and then the girl said, 'I have some good news and some bad news.'"

I could imagine how such a statement would strike fear into a breeder's heart.

"I took a deep breath," Jan resumed, "and said, 'Yes-s-s-s, what is it?' The girl replied, 'Well, the big bird is fine, but I am sorry to tell you the little bird has died!'"

The Hobo arrived on schedule the next day and, so far, has stayed in one place. Inevitably Jim changed her name to match his favorite surfboard.

When fall came, Jim moved Hobie upstairs to his home office. Hobie enjoyed sitting on the back of his office chair, peering at the computer screen over his shoulder. When things got slow, she would groom Jim by nibbling tufts of his hair. And when she decided it was dinnertime, she would spread her wings and begin beating them. Big gyrfalcon wings can produce quite a bit of breeze. It's a bit like being in a wind tunnel. The papers on Jim's desk would fly about, and it became impossible to ignore her.

Early the next spring our granddaughter, Neave, came to spend a week of school vacation with us. She climbed the stairs one morning to visit her grandfather in his attic office. "Grandpa! What is that bird doing here?" she exclaimed.

Hobie was not used to strangers coming into her quarters. She began to shriek at Neave. Neave, in turn, was not used to one of our birds being so rude to her. The immediate result was she was no fonder of Hobie than Hobie was of her.

"Well, she lives here in my office, Neave," Jim explained. "She is an imprint falcon and she thinks she is my mate."

"Grandpa!" The nine-year-old was scandalized. "You already are married! Gramma is your mate."

"Hobie doesn't think so," Jim laughed.

The episode bothered Neave for her entire visit. "Grandpa should tell the bird he is married," she fretted to me. Just before she went home, she confided to me, "Gramma, you are much better looking than that bird!" This was high praise indeed and something I will always treasure.

CHAPTER 29

Tabasco

I should have explained to Neave that once one of our birds fell in love with me. It's not always birds raised as imprints who focus upon a human as a mate. We had heard it was possible for falconry birds originally from the wild to, over a period of years, fix upon a human as their life partner. We learned this to be true from Tabasco, the old red-tail who was first Jim's apprentice bird and then mine. I had thought on the day a wild red-tailed hawk chased Injun and me into the backyard that Tabasco's shriek was because he saw the wild hawk as an intruder into his area. Now I think what happened may have been Tabasco defending me as his mate.

Whenever I shared a friendly chat with my next-door neighbor in the yard, Tabasco would vocalize a warning from his mew. The same thing would happen if a strange car pulled into the driveway and I approached it to inquire if the driver was looking for someone. Somehow this protective aspect of Tabasco seemed focused on me, not on Jim, who had shared a stronger relationship as a hunter and falconer with the red-tail.

Tabasco's courtship evolved into vocalized entreaties for me to join him in his mew. I politely declined, but when it became evident he was trying both to arrange his floor covering into some sort of structure and to attract me into helping him, I assisted by bringing him tree boughs. Sure enough, he was building a nest! I did not have any notion of how to fend off the advances of a red-tail in love, so I told Jim *he* was the one to go in and out of Tabasco's mew. Although Jim was forever his falconry hunting partner and companion, throughout the rest of his full and lengthy life, Tabasco professed his attraction to me. Like my granddaughter's compliment, it is something I will always treasure.

With his big, bone-crushingly powerful toes equipped with talons that looked like mini-scimitars, Tabasco might have been considered the most potentially dangerous of our birds. And yet, he was one of our sweetest birds to handle. He had the wild bird inhibition of not wanting to touch humans. People jump to the conclusion that because raptors are so good at what they do—being *birds of prey*—they are vicious. But "vicious" connotes being consciously, purposefully dangerous, and premeditation has little to do with raptor behavior.

Are they reactive? Can they inflict harm? The answer is yes, of course. The most dangerous birds are imprinted raptors who regard humans as part of their own species. Birds of prey are not kind to other birds of prey, and their reactions to one another are myriad and complex, none of which has anything to do with viciousness. While Tabasco was most certainly a capable predator, his metabolism was slower than that of a goshawk or Harris's hawk, and he was much less apt to strike out from nervousness or yarak.

During our first time exhibiting at the New Hampshire Fish and Game Department's Discover Wild New Hampshire event, we cordoned off the area for our birds with caution tape and two long tables. But however much care is taken with cordoning off an area with tape and tables, toddlers do not see tables as a barrier. Why should they?

They can walk right under them. This is something that didn't occur to us until later.

It had been a busy day, and partway through Jim was speaking with a young woman who seemed consumed with interest in our birds. As Jim responded to her questions, her eyes suddenly widened as she focused on something behind him. Her eyes and her sharp intake of breath caused us to turn to see what had drawn her attention. Overwhelmed by the birds, she had let go the hand of her young child. The toddler, wanting to get closer to the object of *her* interest, simply walked under one of the tables and straight to Tabasco. We saw the chilling sight of a tiny child standing on her tiptoes with her angelic face poised inches from the talons of nature's ablest predator, about to give Tabasco a big hug. Tabasco was also on tiptoe, stretching as high as he possibly could to avoid the grasp of the child. If a bird could wear an expression of worry, one was written on his face as he looked in our direction. It was a moment that could turn one's blood to ice water. Jim lost not a portion of a second as he lunged for the toddler and swept her up in his arms.

After the incident, Tabasco visibly heaved a sigh and settled back on his perch, relieved from the threat of being grasped by a being so small he wasn't sure it was human. What amazed Jim and me then, and in all the years since, was that the mother never made any noise other than a small gasp. The sensory overload of seeing our birds had rendered her powerless to emit a warning. Had it not been for the expression on her face, Jim and I would not have turned simultaneously. We learned how fixated visitors to our exhibits can become.

We are grateful Tabasco demonstrated his wild hawk instinct by preparing to flee from danger. We knew that he did not take harassment or unpleasantness lightly. For a while, my husband had the habit of lifting his gloved hand, raising his hawk near his face to ruffle the feathers on the back of Tabasco's head with his nose. Obviously Tabasco did not share Jim's enthusiasm for this playful gesture, and the day came when Jim had ruffled his feathers one time too many. Tabasco's beak went up into Jim's nostrils to nip the septum of Jim's nose. Just as the dogs had benefitted from Tabasco's instruction, so did Jim.

Tabasco died at the age of sixteen, a full life for a male red-tailed hawk. It is not unusual for females to live and hunt well into their twenties, but male raptors, just as male humans, usually have a shorter lifespan than their female counterparts.

Tabasco's last day was a normal one, with no evidence of ending any differently. Each day when I fed him, we would play a game. He would call to me as I approached. "Hungry, Tabasco?" I'd say. "Look what I have for you today!" Tabasco's part was to land from his perch with a thump on the floor, then rap at the canvas sheet that hung across the opening until I threw his food in. On his last day, I heard Tabasco land on the other side of the canvas, but no rap followed. Something was wrong. I swept the canvas sheet aside to find Tabasco had tumbled onto his side on the mew floor. For an instant, he struggled to come to me and then he collapsed. I lifted him in my arms and called for Jim in the same moment.

There is something very final when a raptor closes its feathered eyelids over eyes in which the fire has dimmed. Tabasco turned to face me and closed his eyes. He died before Jim could reach us.

CHAPTER 30

Mosby, the Gray Ghost

In the spring and fall, when the balance of light and dark is precisely just right, we hear the calls of an imprinted goshawk in love. The love object is my husband, and the bird calling to him has lived here for fifteen years, a long life for a raptor we thought would surely die when she was only nine and a half weeks old.

We have handled raptors with various backgrounds. Some of them were from the wild; some came from breeders but were raised by their parents (the term for this is "chamber raised"); and some were imprinted from the time they were hatched by breeders. In the case of Tabasco, we learned a non-imprinted bird from the wild could begin to demonstrate imprinted behaviors after a period of years spent with humans. Another thing we've learned is that it is a mistake to try to handle a wild or a chamber-raised bird like you would a bird imprinted from the time it could see, or a bird semi-imprinted over a long association.

To understand the sequence of our accidental imprinting of Mosby, you need to know wild goshawks are, for the most part, shy and nervous as they go about their business of catching small game or birds on the wing and then returning to their homes in the deep woods—unless you approach their nests in the spring, that is. Then you'll hear a loud, staccato scream—*ack, ack, ack, ack, ack!*—warning you to get out of the area. What comes after and sometimes during the calls is a large raptor dive-bombing your head to rake you with its razor-sharp talons.

Jim received a call one spring day from our friend Tom Ricardi, who was the head of the Massachusetts Division of Fisheries and Wildlife's Law Enforcement division. Tom told Jim he had a young goshawk, likely about four and a half weeks old, which had been brought in as a "salvage bird." Tom knew Jim had raised young goshawks before, so his question to Jim was if he wanted to raise this young bird for use as a falconry bird. Of course, the answer was yes, and we hurried to meet Tom in Worcester, Massachusetts. When we got there, Tom told us how the eyass goshawk came to be salvaged.

It was spring turkey hunting season in Massachusetts. A turkey hunter had gone into a forest that was a nesting area for a pair of goshawks. He must have ignored the warning cries, for suddenly he was under attack. The man panicked and fired, resulting in the death of the female goshawk. (We wondered if he had actually shot both parents, or if something had already befallen the male, because there was no remaining parent guarding the nest.) Recovered from his initial panic, the man realized he had done something very wrong. He turned himself in to the Division of Fisheries and Wildlife and offered to guide them to the nest.

When the conservation officers and the hunter reached the nest, they spotted two baby goshawks with no parent birds nearby. When no parent bird returned, a climber went up the next day to bring down the chicks, one male and one female. The male chick was given to a Massachusetts falconer. The female was to come home with us. Tom sent along a cooler full of frozen mice for feeding the eyass hawk. We carefully put the nestling into a cardboard box lined with towels and set the box on the backseat of our car.

We had barely cleared the city limits before the curious young hawk climbed out, found a perch on the top of the seat, and watched the other cars on the road. Knowing goshawks as adults are gray and black, fast, and strike without warning, I suggested the name "Mosby, the Gray Ghost" after the famous Confederate raider and guerilla fighter John Singleton Mosby. Jim was not in favor of the name since his bird was a female, but the name persisted, and she is Mosby still.

It is amazing to watch eyass raptors develop. Up to the age of about four weeks, they are white fuzzballs. At four and a half weeks, a little stubby tail starts poking out and the wings sprout feathertips. The fluff is shed at every grooming, which happens often because new feathers must be itchy. During the next five weeks, startling changes take place. The stubby tail feathers emerge out of the baby hawk's body to form a thirteen- or fourteen-inch tail. The young goshawk now has a pair of fully feathered wings, the longest primary feathers of which are another thirteen or fourteen inches in length. This feather development seems to happen overnight until the fuzzball is completely transformed.

Where do the feathers come from? Well, they are made of calcium derived from what the goshawk eats. We were feeding Mosby mainly the mice Tom had given us, not realizing he may have expected us to supplement them. There wasn't enough bone or calcium in these mice for a creature increasing its size by the feathers it was growing. There is normally a progression of ills that befall a calcium-deprived creature. First, muscle control begins to erode, and then the creature goes blind. Next, the creature begins to have seizures. Its nervous system fails due to insufficient calcium and death occurs. We learned later that the rapid growth of those long feathers was depleting the calcium Jim's young goshawk needed to live.

The problem came on suddenly. "Mosby is not moving right," Jim told me. "She cannot seem to stand up, and I don't think she can see." He was gathering his glove and equipment as he said this, and was out the door on his way to her mew before I could respond. When he brought her in, it was evident there was something terribly wrong. We put her in a box, where she soon began thrashing in a seizure. We looked at one another, our shared thought written on each of our faces. We had a bird near death, and neither of us expected she would survive. I ran for the address book of our falconry contact phone numbers. As I dialed the number of the Vermont Institute of Natural Science Raptor Center, Mosby began thrashing in another seizure.

I was calling our friend Mike Cox, the director of the center and a raptor rehabilitator. We knew we needed his expert help fast. The center receptionist told me Mike was leading a group of bird-watchers on a birding excursion. When I caught my breath and launched into the reason for our call, she put me through to the rehab building. The young woman on the other end of the call explained she was a veterinarian working at the center and lately arrived from West Virginia where she had had just finished treating nine-and-a-half-week-old goshawks for calcium deficiency.

"Go to your farm store," she told me, "and buy bonemeal—the kind you put on your flowers. Pulverize it. Then mince quail meat and mix the bone meal into it. Feed the bird with forceps to get the bonemeal down its throat. Oh! Go to your local pharmacy, too, and pick up electrolytes—the kind you give a sick child. Feed that to the goshawk with a syringe."

I raced to the local feed store to get there before it closed, and then on to the pharmacy to get a big bottle of orange-colored electrolyte mixture. Jim chopped up quail while I was gone. By the time I returned, Mosby was having seizures repeatedly, five or six per hour. It did not seem possible we could save the young gos, but we managed to get a bit of food down her throat and made sure as much bonemeal as possible went along with it. Afterwards we fed her electrolytes by the syringe. She kept the food down, and the electrolytes went down even more easily. She seemed to savor the liquid. After some more feedings, the seizures became fewer and fewer. We turned out the lights for the night and wondered if we would have a live or a dead goshawk in the morning.

The next morning, Mosby was standing upright in the box, although she was still fairly wobbly and most assuredly was blind. The awful seizures had stopped. We took this as a good sign. Every few hours we would give her a feeding, carefully lifting the bonemeal-encrusted quail morsels to her beak with forceps. After each feeding we would fill a small syringe with the orange electrolyte fluid. As soon as the plastic tip of the syringe tapped against her beak, she would open and guzzle the electrolyte solution down, obviously relishing the liquid.

One morning several days later, Mosby came running across the box interior when she saw the syringe. Her sight had returned! Now she was up to eating her food from a dish, so we were able to stop feeding with the forceps. I joked to Jim that he should make a lure with an orange syringe when he began to fly with her. (In fact, when Jim emerged from the house one day with an orange popsicle, she nearly tore her perch from the ground trying to get to him!) Joking was something we could afford to do now that we were both relieved at having seen Mosby through a very onerous period.

The period had effected other changes, which soon became obvious. Mosby watched for us and hurried to join us when we approached. Once she was restored to health and put back into her mew, we were greeted with lots of goshawk vocalizations whenever we stepped into her sightline. This has continued until present day. I often imitate her call and she'll call back. She flies from her high corner perch to a lower perch when she hears Jim entering her mew. There she sits patiently as he inserts each jess through the grommet of her anklets, never bating nor striking out as he handles her. She watches for him and gives excited vocal responses to his appearance.

The next spring, we got irrefutable proof we had an imprinted goshawk. In spring and fall the hours of daylight are just the right amount for goshawk hormones to rage and courting behavior to begin. A courting goshawk puts on one of nature's most striking displays. Mosby lifts her tail and spreads the luxurious white feathers into what looks like a huge chrysanthemum flower. Accepting either one of us as a potential mate, she struts a bit, back and forth, in what I call her best "Sailor, do you come here often?" manner. Her courting behavior has given us an entirely new chapter on what we understood about imprinting. The old falconers' lore about "sealing the eyes" (during the medieval era, master falconers would stitch a falcon's eyelids closed and then remove the stitches after so the falcon's ability to see was regained after this period of time to effect imprinting of the falcon upon the falconer) and hooding raptors for extended periods began to be more understandable to us. We knew that imprinting typically occurs as sight develops in newly hatched birds. But the idea that imprinting could occur if the bird lost sight and then regained it was new to us. Fortunately, during Mosby's battle with calcium deficiency, we must have done everything right.

Mosby is now fifteen years old. We are courted by her twice a year, and her calls usually attract a wild male to hang about outside her mew at least once a season. What could have ended in sadness and disaster has turned out well. I wish I could thank that wonderful young veterinarian who helped us, but I was so panicked at the time, I never thought to ask her name.

CHAPTER 31

Emma's Great Adventure

At one point, I thought it would be a good thing to acquire another lanner falcon for the school. Lanners are from the Mediterranean region and Africa. When I tell people these birds are depicted in Egyptian hieroglyphics and were the models for those striking falcon headdresses worn by the priests, they turn to study my lanners more intently. Once I had lanners, I learned that they often sit perched and at rest with their wings down at their sides, just like the headdresses. In North America, lanners are in constant demand for their characteristically low, compact flights. This makes them desirable for flight exhibitions and for the commercial falconry businesses, known as bird abatement, that use lanners to scare away nuisance birds from airports and farms.

I found a breeder out west who told me he had back orders for the next year or so. "But," he said, "I do have an older female from my breeding stock, which I will sell to you. She is an imprint that has stopped laying, but she should have a few years left for some flying and for use at your school. She is a very sweet bird." The cost was cheaper than getting a young bird, and I could get her right away. I took him up on his offer, sent off my payment, and waited for my new-old lanner to arrive by airline.

I expected a repeat of Mrs. Chicken, but unlike our sweet first lanner, the female from the west was more like a tiger. Make that a saber-toothed tiger. There was no denying she was beautiful, and as a bird for falconry education, she was a good fit—as soon as I could make friends with her, that is.

With the new lanner, I wanted more than just an exotic bird to exhibit. I wanted to fly her and to have her handled by students in my classes. From the onset, it was clear I had my work cut out for me. She had been handled only by her breeder, a man, and she had imprinted on him. So, as far as she was concerned, he was her mate and I was an unwanted intruder. I did not even get to choose her name. Jim told me because I had named Mosby, I owed him one. He chose "Emma Peel," a character from the 1960s television series *The Avengers*.

When I had her coming from the perch to the lure and then to the glove, I figured I was making progress, despite her suspicious glares throughout the procedure. Emma was larger than Mrs. Chicken, which made it difficult to judge her correct weight for flying. The day came when I decided to test her using a creance line. She came directly on the call twice. With a deep breath, I took the plunge and released her from the creance. I placed her on one of the upright granite posts at the perimeter of the yard, stepped away a few paces, turned, and whistled her in. Then all hell broke loose.

Instead of a sedate Mrs. Chicken, I had something zooming about me in small circles, attempting to break the sound barrier. Emma Peel widened her circle to career around the house and then back over me. She barely glanced down as I whistled and swung the lure. Then she took herself off into the sky. I ran to the house to load the lure with a whole quail that I had defrosting on the kitchen counter.

I walked the perimeters of the front and back yards, whistling and swinging the quail-laden lure. As I completed my first circle, the knot with which I had hastily tied the quail to the lure let loose and the quail sailed through the air to land in a large patch of thickly growing ferns. *Drat!* I searched the fern patch but could not find the quail. *Well, no matter*, I told myself. Just as I stepped out of the fern patch, Mrs. Peel flew down into it to retrieve the quail. She had, unbeknownst to me, been sitting on a tree limb all the while, and her keen eyesight had seen exactly where the quail had landed. In a flash she grabbed it and was off again, carrying her prize. *Double drat!*

This was the last I saw of Emma Peel until two mornings later when she took off out of the oak tree by the back door as I exited the house to get the morning paper. Jim and I wondered how long she would last in the great outdoors. Emma had lived her entire twelve years in a small chamber looking out at a patch of blue sky. She had grabbed her opportunity for high adventure, and we were worried an out-of-condition, "unwild" falcon could not last long without falling victim to an owl, hawk, or some other predator. I continued to search, whistle, and swing lures, but there was no response from the empty sky.

On the fourth day that Emma went missing, we were scheduled to give a class for the Fish and Game Department's "Becoming an Outdoors Woman" program at Squam Lakes. I guessed that Emma might come back to our house or some other human habitation after the quail was out of her system. I left word with the police dispatcher that our tame falcon was on the loose and might seek out humans for food. I requested the police call my home number to leave a message if someone saw the falcon.

While we packed the car and loaded our birds, I kept listening for the phone to ring. Once on the road, I used my cell phone to call home to check for messages. Nothing. Just before we left the cabin to go eat supper in the dining hall, I checked again. Nothing. After supper, with the sun sinking over Squam Lake, we returned to our cabin and I checked once more.

"Mrs. Cowan," the voice on my machine said, "please call the Hillsboro PD. I believe we have your bird here."

My heart lurched. Was she alive? Was she dead? Was she injured? I couldn't dial the number fast enough. The dispatcher relayed my call to the officer who had left the message.

"I think we have your bird here. We got a call from the mobile home park down by the river when it flew into a lady's yard yesterday. When it was still there today, the lady called us again. She knew the bird belonged to someone because it was so tame, and it had straps on its legs. After she called, the lady went outside and scooped the bird into a cat carrier. We went over and picked it up. We have it here in the carrier and it seems fine. Is this your bird?"

I explained we could not get to Hillsboro before two in the afternoon of the next day. The policewoman was concerned about leaving the bird in the carrier, but I said it was the safest place for the falcon until we could redeem her at the station.

Her next concern was whether the falcon needed food or water. "No, don't give her anything," I told her. "Be sure everyone knows not to feed her anything. You can kill her if you feed her something she should not have. Just keep her in a quiet spot until we can get there tomorrow."

I was elated Emma Peel was in captivity again, but I couldn't put my anxiety for her well-being to rest. As soon as we finished teaching our class the next morning, we were on the road again, and just before two o'clock we entered the Hillsboro PD parking lot. Two police officers escorted us to where they were keeping the falcon. I suspected the second officer was along out of curiosity. It was obvious that having Emma Peel in "lockup" had caused quite a stir in the department.

"We are keeping the bird in the bay," one of the officers said. They led us to the garage where the fire engines and rescue vehicles were normally kept. When one of the officers pushed a button to open the door, we saw nothing but a small animal carrier in the cavernous emergency vehicle bay. The tiny box looked impossibly incongruous sitting all alone on the floor of the garage.

I had pulled my falconry glove from our car as I got out. In it I held a whole dead quail I had taken from the cooler in the car. If I was correct, Mrs. Peel had not eaten in quite a while, and I figured she would be ravenous. "Well, are you hungry, Mrs. Peel?" I said as we stepped into the huge bay. As soon as I said this, the cat carrier began to rock wildly back and forth and make little hops off the ground.

The police officers were wide-eyed at the phenomenon. "I think the bird is glad to see you," one of them said.

I knelt by the carrier, opened the door a crack, and stuck the quail into the opening. Immediately, two sets of talons clamped down on it. I withdrew my glove with Emma riding upon it and attached my leash to her jesses with my free hand. As Emma tore into the quail carcass, I raised her up so the officers could get a clear view of "the perpetrator" they had been keeping in custody. I was thrilled she seemed no worse for wear from her sojourn. *But what was that smell?* The stench that hit our nostrils caused Jim and me to gag.

"Good Lord," I finally managed to say. "What is that awful smell?" It was like the worst cat odor imaginable combined with an undetermined pungency. The officers looked chagrined.

"We told him you said not to," one of them said sheepishly.

"Yeah, we told him he shouldn't do it," the other volunteered. I looked at the pair in puzzlement. I was beginning to see the reasoning behind putting the carrier in an empty garage. Likely, the rescue vehicles had been removed to protect them from absorbing the odor.

"Not do what?" Jim inquired, averting his nose.

"It was the chief," one of the policemen explained. "He was afraid the bird was hungry, so he tried to feed it his tuna fish sandwich."

"Oh, my God, no!" Jim said. "If she had eaten it, it could have killed her!" The confession caused us both to examine Mrs. Peel more closely. The evidence was there. She was smeared with a mix of greasy dried mayonnaise and flecks of tuna fish. The officers were now red-faced with embarrassment.

"Well, I don't think she ate any of it, which is a good thing, so we probably don't have to worry," I reassured them. "But, for future reference, tell the chief that feeding a falcon something it should not have, like cooked or greasy food, is a good way to kill it"

We thanked the pair profusely and started for home, but not before opening the car windows first. I hooded Mrs. Peel, who by now had a crop full of quail and was resting happily on my glove. The other birds, still in the car from the trip to Squam Lake, and Emma herself were not bothered by the vile odor because they have practically no sense of smell. When we got home, the first order of business was a bath for Emma Peel before she was put away in her mew.

The lasting result of Emma's adventure was that she transferred all her imprinting love to Jim and me. She settled in and became a wonderful bird for us and for our students to handle. Later, when I chanced to speak to the breeder, I told him all about Emma's great adventure. He was pleased she had taken a sabbatical to fly about for a bit after having produced twenty-five chicks for him. And I was glad Emma Peel and I had reached a level where we took pleasure in one another's company.

CHAPTER 32

Jazz

One year, after the club had closed for the winter, Jim and I brought a fellow falconer to Timberdoodle on an abnormally warm December afternoon to hunt game birds. There had been pheasants everywhere, making the day a perfect conclusion to what was nearing the end of the upland bird season. Clouds were gathering and I suspected a winter storm was brewing, so I was anxious to get Jazz, my big female Harris's hawk, into the air.

After I launched her off my glove, she kept pace with us, moving from tree to tree, as our friend, Jim, and I walked towards a pond where I knew pheasants often gathered. Just as we came to a bend in the lane, two pheasants flushed from high in a tree at the road's edge where they were roosted. At the same time, on the opposite side of the road, Jazz launched from a tree limb on a level with the pheasants. One pheasant was on a collision course with my hawk. The two birds met nearly head to head. My pulse was hammering with anticipation of what would surely end as a quick take of the game bird or an exciting chase.

Instead, Jazz turned off, refusing to meet her prey. I was dumbfounded, Jim was disappointed, and our friend was philosophical. "Sometimes it happens like that. There was a reason she turned away. We just don't know what it is," he said in answer to Jim's snort of disgust. I called Jazz down as we prepared to leave. My puzzlement was total. Jazz was usually righteous about catching prey. Why had she pulled out of what would surely have been a take?

I acquired Jazz because I wanted a larger hawk to fly on pheasants. Injun was not sizable enough to hold his own with those big game birds, although he loved catching them and had developed some clever ways to do so. About ten days after Jazz had arrived, Injun lay dead in his mew at eleven years of age. I was devastated over losing him. It was not until the next year's hunting season that I would hunt with Jazz.

The first time I flushed prey for her at Timberdoodle, a game bird rose straight into the air about fifty feet. Jazz took flight to hit it at the apex of its rise, at which time the two birds veered apart. Jazz went one direction while the hen pheasant went the other direction, fleeing from my hawk. I had three hunters in the field standing alongside me watching. They were amazed, despite the escape of the pheasant, at the display of flying prowess from my young bird. I turned to them with a slight smile, knowing that bitter disappointment was felt by Jazz. "She won't let that happen again," I told them. "I will bet you she is very unhappy the game bird got away." What I said proved to be true. Jazz became a wonderful hunting hawk. She anticipated the escape strategies of her prey and matched them with her powerful flights. She was one of the most successful hunters it has been my privilege to work alongside.

Taking game is undeniably a high point to share with your bird. Some falconers keep a head count of the number of game birds taken by their birds. I am not a head count person. The moments when my bird is in pursuit provide pure, heart-thumping excitement. If my bird is successful, it indicates I have done my part in helping to find game, in conditioning, and in maintaining my raptor properly. My best days are when the bird and I have had a great day hunting and go home together safe and sound no matter the head count, although, I have to admit, when Jazz took three head of game in three separate flights one day, it was a very proud day for me.

I was full of anticipation when we began Jazz's fifth hunting season. My bird had been improving every year, but something had changed. She was her old self when I put her on quail or medium-size quarry, but she would pull out of long, hard-driving pursuits on pheasants. This had been one of her strong suits in previous years. Finally came the day she met that cock pheasant face to face in the air and turned away without even trying to take him. She was different, too, in her manner—more passive and quieter. At the same time, she was feather-perfect, in good flesh, and eating well. Perhaps, I theorized, my bird, now in her fifth year, was changing hormonally. She was my first female Harris's. I had no experience with brooding hens. I wondered if she would attempt nesting and egg laying in the spring.

One day in early March, I stepped into her mew to find her on the floor and in distress. I picked her up, cradling her in my arms as I ran to the house shouting for Jim. She was dead by the time I got in the door. Examining her more closely, I saw that she had not expelled her feces with enough force to clear her tail and her feathers were smeared with the fresh mutes. Had I done something wrong? I could not get the question out of my brain.

We decided to have her autopsied. I needed to protect the other raptors on our property, if necessary, from whatever killed my bird in her prime. The first thing I did was call Tufts Wildlife Clinic in Massachusetts to find if there were any maladies that could strike down a seemingly healthy bird in such a way. I spoke with a doctor there who went over various diseases and symptoms, none of which fit the situation. He concurred that a necropsy should be done by a local veterinarian. "Be sure to send tissue samples to Northwest ZooPath, though," he said. "They are the best at analyzing and reporting on raptor tissue."

I made an appointment with Mike Dutton, the vet who worked with me in raptor rehabilitation. Upon arrival, Mike made short work of preparing for the procedure. My heart lurched at the ripping sound as he plucked breast feathers from Jazz's body prior to making the incision. I had steeled myself for what was to come, but the sound had been unexpected and it hit me like a blow. I reminded myself the fierce, bright flame that had been Jazz was now gone. The carcass remaining was like a cold candlewick after the glow and the heat have gone out of it.

Once the body was opened, Dr. Dutton probed her organs, explaining which was which. "But this is very odd," he said. "Look here. The liver seems to be growing all over the place." What he had found was oddly checkered tissue. It was a growth from the liver with thousands of tendrils going in and out, around organs, filling every possible space within the body cavity. Dutton took photos and sample tissue. It all was sent off to the zoo-pathology laboratory. Within three weeks, we had a report back.

I was stunned at the diagnosis. I was used to learning things that made raptors different from humans. Now as I read the pathology report, I was learning that a disease that had taken a favorite cousin who was like a sister . . . had taken Jazz as well.

Jazz had developed a cancerous tumor on her liver that had filled every nook and every cranny of her body and halted her metabolism. It was like a clock stops when something is jammed in its works. I had done nothing wrong, but this did not make me feel better. Instead, I was depressed. Even by doing everything right, my bird had died. The weight of failure was resting on my shoulders. I mulled over how Jazz had changed, little by little, through the months of the previous fall and winter. Now I understood why Jazz had become quiet and why, as the season ended, she had pulled away from the pursuit of big pheasants she had neither the power nor the breath to catch and kill. There never was a quelling of her hunting drive, but, simply, the physical mechanisms of her body were not able to serve her magnificent instincts.

I called the doctor at Tufts to tell him the results of the lab report. "I did not know raptors could get cancer," I blurted out.

"Nancy, every living thing can get cancer," he said. This was the lesson I wished I had never had the opportunity to learn.

Losing Injun and then Jazz left me feeling empty and remorseful. But life here with our birds does not allow us to dwell on the bad. Things go on, and the fact was I had just begun the falconry school. I either had to move forward or give up on the idea of running the school, something in which I had already invested a great many hours and much effort.

I allowed myself the summer to get reorganized and get the school equipped with a new hawk. Working with the falcons was very good therapy. The steady, disciplined regimen of training has a sweetness that heals unhappiness. And when a new, young Harris's hawk arrived, I threw myself into training with the new bird. The depression faded and life began to hum at a normal pace.

CHAPTER 33

Lightning in a Bottle

Besides utilizing the summer to work with falcons, summer is the period when we most often end up rehabbing young raptors from the wild, such as the merlin, Swifty. Although we mainly rehab falcons, on one occasion we were called upon to rehabilitate an eyass goshawk. Here was new territory for me. Jim had raised and trained goshawks, but I had not. When it was proposed to us, I jumped at the opportunity.

His name was 3-D, named, like N-Z had been, from the identification markings on his leg band. His nest had been monitored by Department of the Interior personnel involved in a research project mapping habitats, which included the banding of young goshawks. Mariko Yamasaki, the wildlife biologist in charge of the survey, was concerned this tiercel eyass was so small that his three sisters would likely outcompete him for food. As she had suspected, a few days after 3-D was banded, he was pushed from the nest to the ground below either by his parents or by his squabbling siblings. An intern from the project retrieved him, and he was brought to us.

Some years prior, a Maine falconer named Eric Wilcox had corrected my stance when I called Injun to my glove. "Like this," he said, turning me around so my back was to my bird. "Then raise your glove." Eric explained that if I faced the raptor I was calling, I was leaving my face largely unprotected. And if I went on to take up flying goshawks, he warned, a stance in which I faced an oncoming bird left me with no defense should the bird suddenly veer towards my eyes. With goshawks, this is a very real possibility.

Eric did not have to explain the propensity of goshawks to "go for the eyes." I already knew all about it. Jim had explained years before that if anything seemed different or out-of-sync to a goshawk, it would prompt the bird to grab for the head. Hawks kill by having their talons penetrate the heart or the brain of their prey, and Eric had warned me that many falconers who flew goshawks were marked by the scars on their faces. Eyes, to goshawks, are nature's bull's-eye targets.

Goshawks are superlative flyers, surpassed only by the two smaller types of the three accipiters, the Cooper's hawk and the sharp-shinned hawk. These three accipiters are known as bird-catchers and are the woodland aero-acrobats. Skill and agility combine with hair-trigger reactions to produce the equivalent of flying "live wires." With their wonderful abilities to catch prey and their mercurial attention spans, these accipiters require more expertise from falconers.

In the world of the goshawk, the equation is simple (it has to be, to match their short-circuited, tiny lump of gray matter): "If something, anything, differs during the flight on game, you must be losing food. If you are losing food, go for the eyes." Goshawks are never very particular as to which set of eyes they go for. If the human calling them has the nearest set of eyes when they realize food may be missing, the human's face can become the target.

My first lesson on this topic came with Jim's female goshawk, Thistle. Jim had been telling me how calm she was and how easy to handle in the mew. One night we were going out to supper to celebrate our anniversary. "Would you feed Thistle for me?" Jim asked me. "I want to take a shower and change before we go out." Jim always hand-fed Thistle himself.

"You have to tell me *exactly* what to do," I said warily. I had a healthy respect for what Jim, Eric, and other falconers had told me about goshawks.

"It's easy. You hold out the first chick on the glove. She jumps for it, eats, and jumps back to the perch. Do that with each of the three chicks. That's all there is to it."

So, my husband went in for his shower and I went off to the goshawk's mew, like a lamb to slaughter. Thistle barely seemed surprised it was me entering her mew. I fed her one chick, a second chick, and then a third just as Jim had told me. After the third feed on the glove, Thistle jumped back to her perch. She turned to look at me as I pivoted and took a step towards the door. The next thing I felt was a talon curving into the corner of my eye, just about to encircle my eyeball. In a split second, I remember hoping she would not grasp, as she would surely remove my eye. Instead, she struck at my face with her foot and darted back to a corner of the mew.

I flew out the door, slammed it shut behind me, and leaned back against it to gather my wits and catch my breath. I had blood running down my face from the puncture and slash below my eye. My face began to throb as the swelling set in. The fact that I still possessed two eyes and could see out of each made me extremely grateful. However, I was ready to throttle one particular individual. The object of my rage, now freshly showered and attired, burst out of the house and ran to me.

"Oh, no! I will never ask you to feed one of my goshawks again! I am so sorry. Are you all right?" asked the Jim.

"*What* didn't you tell me?" My words hung in the air with icicles dripping from each.

"Huh?"

"What did you *not tell me*? What did you *not* tell me to do that I should have done, because *something* was different and she did *not* like it?!!"

"Well, did you do what I told you?"

I explained exactly what I had done, thrice, which was exactly what he had told me to do.

"Oh," he said. "I forgot." He paused a moment and then continued, "After I feed her the third chick and before I leave the mew, I reach out and go *fluffle-fluffle* to Thistle's breast feathers so she will never be hand-shy." Concern and chagrin were written on my husband's face.

I stood in silence for a moment after his disclosure. His afterthought soothed the anger boiling inside me. In fact, I had to smile at the thought of my macho-Marine husband doing anything like a *fluffle-fluffle*. The humor of the situation saved the day. At dinner Jim explained to the waitress and restaurant owner he had not caused my Technicolor shiner. At least, not directly. From that point forward, I knew to beware for the sake of my eyes whenever handling a goshawk.

3-D was nowhere near the size of Thistle, but once he was past the fluff-ball stage, his ability to inflict damage was at full capacity. His long, curved talons were needle sharp, and the power in his feet made them as dangerous as daggers. When he was fully feathered and ready to begin training so I could get him hunting on his own, Jim and I put anklets on him. During the process, I released a hold on one of his feet to better my grip. This was a costly error. In a flash, my wrist was encircled by talons sunk in to the hilt. I felt the bones inside my wrist bumping against one another as 3-D's talons pierced from either side and slid between them. Jim had to pry each talon out, as 3-D had no intention of letting go. When I was finally free, my knees went weak, and I sat down. This episode permanently impaired the use of my thumb on my right hand.

Once he was equipped with anklets, my training with 3-D commenced. He was very responsive to the whistle and took to the flying lure very naturally—hardly a surprise given the excellent predators goshawks are. With the first time on game, I made the mistake of trying to fly him as if he thought like a Harris's hawk. He took a perfect perch in a tree, and I did the perfect flush of a quail, which flew right under his perch. 3-D was by then looking in the other direction, and the quail flew off into the woods. I had heard about the short attention span of a goshawk, something I have since decided is no wider than a hair on a nanosecond. Goshawks are frequently flown directly from the glove, and 3-D was the perfect example of why that is so.

One day, I was flying 3-D when he took a perch in the cedar tree behind our house. A small finch landed in the tree as well, and 3-D spotted it. Then the chase was on. Around and around the trunk, under the cover of the needles and limbs the pair flew. Their circular flight began to spiral higher and higher within the expanse of the tree. I could just catch a glimpse now and then of the frantic finch trying to outdistance the hawk. Finally the pair reached the top of the pointed cedar and exploded out of it. The finch came out the treetop straight up, as though shot from a cannon. 3-D was within mere fractions of catching the small bird. I blew my whistle and swung my lure at that moment, and 3-D's attention was instantly diverted. He looked down over his wing, saw the lure, and turned to dive for it. The finch escaped to the deep woods, where I'm sure it spent the rest of the day telling the other finches of its narrow escape from the "talons of death." I had never seen such a fast chase by a hawk, or one so constricted in space.

Naturally, I heeded Eric's advice every time I called 3-D to my glove. There was just one problem, though: The closer 3-D got to me, the more his trajectory changed from landing on my glove to—guess where—my eyes! If one were to draw an imaginary line along the trajectory of his approach, his landing spot ended up somewhere around my forehead. I started wondering why Eric hadn't also recommended wearing a hockey goalie's mask. Now I was no longer heeding his advice or, for that matter, any other falconry technique I had learned. It had become, flat out, run for the hills and every woman for herself—backwards! Facing the incoming tiercel, I developed an interesting style of running in reverse as the bird approached and raising my glove higher and higher to keep it on a course of interception with 3-D's flight path. Once 3-D was on my glove and my eyes and other body parts were safe, I was panting and out of breath. The experience was an invigorating adrenaline rush.

As odd as my handling of the young goshawk might have appeared to bystanders, the experience was teaching me reams about accipiters. There was no question in my mind of the superiority of an accipiter over a Harris's where speed and agility were concerned. The hunting drive was even more powerful in 3-D's small body than it had been in Jazz's, whose weight was more than double. Flying 3-D was, absolutely, like uncorking and then flying "lightning in a bottle."

CHAPTER 34

Sidekick

When Jazz died from cancer, I was left without a Harris's hawk. I contacted a breeder named Luis and arranged to get a male from his spring hatch. I brought home the fine young bird I named Scout. I asked Luis to put me down for another Harris's hawk as soon as one was available. Later in the summer, Luis called with news he had another male if I wanted it. The bird was one he had removed early from the breeding chamber so as to have the parent birds hormonally recycle to produce a third clutch that season. Removing a Harris's before its parents cast it out of the nest is not a good plan, I knew, but Luis assured me this was a very friendly bird which would be a cinch to train as it was so accustomed to people.

"It is a full brother to the male you bought earlier, but eight weeks younger," Luis said. "I took it out of the chamber when it was just a brancher." A brancher is a bird in the pre-fledging stage that hops and jumps from place to place with a small assist from its wings. "It lived in a tree by my house and would jump back and forth between the tree and the roof. When I went out, I would throw food down for it. You will like this bird. He will train easy."

In looks and size, the new juvenile Harris's was identical to Scout, so I named him "Sidekick." But there were some very distinct differences between the brothers. For one thing, as soon as he was trained, Sidekick began cowring at me. "Cowring" is an old falconry term and is the action of a young bird showing obedience to an adult. The youngster lowers his body and half-spreads his wings before what he perceives to be the parent. He flutters his wings as he does this. We might call this "cowering," but it is more a submissive gesture than one based on fear. Sometimes, once my juvenile Harris's hawks are trained, there is transference of parenthood status to me and occasionally a manifestation of this cowring behavior. Sidekick started to display cowring to me all the time. The behavior was an omen of what was to come.

From the start the youngster vocalized almost constantly when he was on the glove. Food-begging vocalization in raptors is a real attention get-ter, as it is meant to be. It's especially ear piercing when the bird is right at your side. Falconer friends with whom I hunted called him "The Smoke-Detector" because of the volume and intensity of his screams. I called him "Tyrannosaurus Rex," and you will understand why as I describe what it was like to handle this bird.

While Scout behaved like a properly raised falconry hawk, his brother Sidekick was a hooligan. Scout loathed landing anywhere but on the glove. Touch a human? *Eeuuwwww*. He wanted no part of that! As I began Sidekick's training, I never knew where he would land. Some-times it was my shoulder. Sometimes it was my arm above the glove. He even landed on my head once or twice. As a famous comedian put it some years back, I got no respect. Because he had no fear of human-kind, there was more bad behavior with which I had to contend. When-ever I reached up to take hold of his jesses, or for any other reason, his foot would snatch out at me, and I would be sliced or punctured. My right hand began to resemble hamburger. In short, it was like handling a twenty-one ounce tyrannosaur.

After a week of this, I decided to call Luis. "Luis, did you sell me an imprint?"

"No, Nancy. That bird was never imprinted."

I explained some of the difficulties I was experiencing, but Luis just chuckled. "Keep working with him, Nancy. You will work it out. He will be a fine bird for you."

I hung up muttering imprecations at bird breeders in general and Luis in particular. Later I described the bird to my friend, falconer and wildlife biologist Bruce Haak. I told him what Luis had told me. "Not an imprint? Well then, it is a *mis*-print!" was Bruce's reply.

I went back to training Sidekick, took him hunting, and even introduced him to working with the dog. All in all, he was a poster child for arrested development. But I had worked with birds like him before. Jazz, for example, had had the same inclination as Sidekick to foot me, making a grab and connecting with her talons every time my hand came near her. This undoubtedly had much to do with the fact that the breeder had taken her away from her parents and left her to raise herself in a process called "sibling imprinting," a term that probably meant more to the breeder than it did to me as the falconer having to deal with the footing problem. Sibling imprinting is supposedly when young birds are taken early from their parents to grow up in an environment with their own kind or their siblings.

Raptors are a great example of how the maturation process works. Over the years we've observed them grow up according to the experiences they have had. Parent-raised birds are prepared by their experiences to adopt behaviors that allow them to leave the nest and function on their own. A raptor that is taken away from its parents too young has a slower rate of maturation. And, as is often the case with full imprints, sometimes these birds never quite get over seeing a human as a parent, which is why the falconer must take care not to raise the bird in a manner that will lead it to interact in dangerous ways with humans, most notably hand-feeding when the appealing little fluff-ball shows no resemblance to the terrifying *Tyrannosaurus rex* a badly imprinted raptor will resemble when grown. These mishandling mistakes are responsible for the instances in which humans are most likely to be attacked or injured. Raptors often strike out at their own kind, whether siblings or intruder birds. The imprint bird sees the human as another just like him.

With Jazz, who may have been another "misprint," I found the maturation process was painfully (pun intended) slow compared to what parent birds could accomplish in a matter of days. So I decided to do some reading on the subject. In the case of Harris's hawks, the general advice was never to take one that had been prematurely removed from the care of its parents. With Jazz, I worked out my own solution. *Could I overcome the problem with Sidekick?* I wondered.

The first thing I tried with Sidekick was what I had done with Jazz. Female Harris's hawks are known for their companionable nature with humans. To put it unscientifically, female Harris's seem more apt to care if you are mad at them. Whenever Jazz would foot me, I'd shout the words "No! Hand!" at her. The short *a* in "hand" makes it sound much like a Harris's warning scream, especially when you shout it angrily. This explosive noise adequately expressed to Jazz I was dissatisfied with her, and it did, in fact, discourage her from striking out at me. Throughout the first season, I did this negative shout many times until she stopped footing me. The problem disappeared entirely during the second season except for when Jazz was very excited, and by then she never broke the skin or hurt me. As we began our third season, I had a fine hunting hawk that was, as much as any other good hawk, a pleasure to fly.

Naturally, this was the first technique I tried on Sidekick. By the time I was done, I had screamed everything in the book at him, but to no avail.

Sidekick did not care whether I was angry at him. I guess male Harris's are not as companionable as females.

I had to find something else that would dissuade him from continually striking at me, but it had to be not so negative that he would associate it with *me*. Jim had once taught me a falconry remedy for a falcon that has the bad habit of biting. The best part of it is the falcon never associates the action with the falconer, but instead associates it with the behavior. From long ago, falconers would fill their cheeks with water. When the falcon's head snaked out to bite, the falconer would spritz a fine spray of water from his lips straight into the falcon's face. The trick is to use only a bit of the water each time so the action can be repeated immediately when the falcon attempts to bite again. The hardest part for me has always been to keep enough water in my mouth to spray repeatedly. But I had used the method successfully.

There was a major problem with using this method with Sidekick. While working with him, I would be moving constantly over rough ground and using my whistle. Whereas when I tried this method with a falcon, I could sit still with a glass of water at my side for constant replenishment. Was there anything else Sidekick would dislike enough to stop spearing my hand with his talons but not associate with me, his falconer?

Finally, I found my solution. The times Sidekick would foot me were when he was sitting on the glove and I happened to reach up. Whenever he would strike, my new solution was to free my hand as I shouted and grab his beak, giving it a vigorous shaking. He disliked that intensely. He would wiggle to get his beak free of my fingers. All the while, the nictitating membranes, which are third eyelids that protect the raptor's eyes, would be flashing up and down like crazy window shades. Afterwards, he'd give his head a shake as if to clear it from the distasteful sensation, but I got no menacing postures or screams. He was not associating the beak shake with me.

After two years of enduring his attacks, it only took two days of beak shakes whenever the occasion arose. Now I have a dependable hawk who's much more connected to me than his more independent brother Scout. Another side benefit was that he also stopped screaming for food, a change greeted with relief by everyone within hearing range. In Luis's words, he has made a fine hawk for me! (So much so that I would go on to purchase two more Harris's hawks—two sisters I named Smoke and Fire—from him.)

Having solved the problem of Sidekick's immature behavior, I now had two male Harris's hawks no longer exhibiting marked differences in behavior. Fellow falconers and students were impressed at my ability to discern one from the other. Finally someone asked me by what seemingly invisible means could I know which hawk was which? "Oh, it is easy," I answered. "Scout is a 'righty' and Side is a 'lefty.'"

"That's amazing!" was the speaker's response. "Do you mean to say hawks are 'right-handed' or 'left-handed'?"

At that point, I had to make a full confession. "No," I said, laughing. "Scout's leg band is on his right leg, while Sidekick's is on his left."

CHAPTER 35

Winterizing Harris's Hawks

What do you do with a Harris's hawk, a species native to the southwestern deserts of North America, when winter temperatures in New England drop severely below freezing? The first winter with Injun, I adhered to advice that Harris's hawks should be protected from cold nights when the thermometer went down to the single digits. I kept a weather eye on the thermometer and hauled Injun into the family room when it went below ten degrees at night. I had been told he could withstand low temperatures during the day with no ill effects. I followed the advice carefully.

When the spring came, I noticed several white dots on some of Injun's talons. When I tossed out the lure for him, he came down to hit it with a resounding smack. To my horror, there was blood welling from his talon where it had broken off. He looked down, saw the red blood, and mistook it for a tidbit. He then began to tear at his own foot. I got him home and found styptic powder to staunch the bleeding. The incident scared me badly. Immediately I went into action to find out what had caused the talon to break. I learned the white spots were where the material of the talon had become delaminated, indicating Injun had suffered frostbite to the quick of his talon. What had happened was a wake-up call and changed how I manage Harris's hawks during the winter months.

When hawks get cold, they warm their feet by tucking them up into their feathers, alternating them one foot at a time. The problem with Harris's is that, being native to the deserts of the United States and Mexico, they do not have as much feather insulation as raptors native to the Northeast. The first sign of trouble is the delamination spots. Those spots damaged by frostbite do not form a solid talon, which is made up of layers of keratin. This is why Injun's talon had broken off when he whacked the lure. The bleeding came from breaking the talon too close to a blood vessel, just as would happen to you from breaking a fingernail too close to the quick. If the frostbite had been severe, the entire foot could turn black and drop off. I watched Injun's toes carefully, hoping such a horrible thing would not occur. After another month when I had seen no changes to his feet, I breathed a relieved sigh.

I set a new standard for myself in protecting Injun from the winter temperatures, and this is what I have done for over twenty years since. If the nighttime temperature was forecast to drop below twenty degrees Fahrenheit, my bird came indoors.

Today, I protect my Harris's from the winter elements as I first learned to do with Injun. The only problem is now I have four Harris's hawks to protect from cold temperatures. Rather than invade our living quarters, I bring them to the cellar, which is clean, brightly lit, and fairly spacious. I had a carpenter build stalls that are open on one side, much like the cubicles in office buildings. Each Harris's has its own stall and perch within it. Because our hot water pipes, which pass through the room, are insulated, the temperature stays between forty-five and fifty degrees. It is a perfect place to keep four Harris's hawks from exposure to frigid temperatures. Except for one thing—they get bored.

An idle hawk is the devil's playground, I have learned. I switch the placement of each hawk, give them bath pans with fresh water for bathing, and do all the things I can think of to keep them reasonably occupied and not on the lookout for trouble. One long winter, however, trouble came in several forms.

Smoke and Fire, two sisters from Luis after Scout and Sidekick, started sliding their perches inch by inch across the concrete floor. And their intentions were not friendly, as they are terrifically predatory towards one another. I retaliated by weighting the perches with bricks. I thought the two brothers, Scout and Sidekick, because they lived together in a single mew when they were outside, would deal well with being next to one another. At least they would not try to move their perches. I was wrong. In their boredom, they made life more interesting by engaging in foot fights underneath the partition that separated them. I had not thought an inch and a half of space would allow the boys to get into trouble. But when I went down to feed them one afternoon, I discovered both had scratches to their toes. Alarmingly, Scout had a big chunk out of one toe, and his entire foot had swollen badly. I called the vet, put Scout into the giant hood, and set off for the Fisherville Animal Hospital and Bird Clinic in Concord.

Once there, Dr. George Messenger reached for Scout's foot. Dr. Messenger's interest in avian species means he goes the extra mile to provide the best care for our birds. Even so, Scout was not sure he wanted the white-coated stranger touching his foot.

"Hold on, Doc," I said. Scout was on the glove on my left hand. I encircled him with my right arm so that my right hand could grasp his foot out for the doctor to examine and treat. Scout put up with all this very well and actually settled into my body like a young bird under the protective wing of an adult. This evidence of trust amazed the veterinarian. "Well," Dr. Messenger said. "Come to Momma!"

I did not tell him that it's my practice to pull my coat over my hawks during winter hunts if a stinging wind kicks up. My hawks now associate this maneuver with protection from the elements and therefore are at ease when I pull one close under my arm. Scout's vet visit was accomplished in timely fashion. Not all hawks and falcons would be able to trust being held so close. I was able to do this because Scout was, after all, a Harris's hawk.

Antibiotics and fresh dressings soon healed Scout's wound. My first order of business when we got home was to hawk-proof the cellar by covering the spaces underneath the partitions and weighting everybody's perches even more. Fortunately, for the rest of the winter, hawk activities were limited to Harris's croaking songfests. This made watching and hearing the evening news a challenge, but it was better than having the hawks get into mischief.

CHAPTER 36

Making In

"Watch out!!" My startled clients leap aside, clearing a path for a game bird closely pursued by my big hawk as the pair comes flying through the knot of people.

Smoke is at her best, doing what she is born to do. The flight of a hawk on game is often so fast and far away that few people are privileged to see it up close, but this chase has come to them right at hip level. As Smoke's chase takes her into a patch of woods, I am running after her, leaving the group I am guiding. They must follow me as I try to keep abreast of the sequence of events. Knowing my hawk, this is a race she will win. She will overcome the chukar as it dives into deep cover. She will make her kill.

Now I must find her in the shoulder-high brush. She will not welcome me. Her wings will convulsively flex to arch over the kill, hiding it from sight. But despite her possessiveness, she will trust me as I kneel to retrieve her jesses, slide my glove beneath the dead game bird, and lift it with Smokey firmly attached, her talons driven deeply into her prey, her wings mantled over her kill and my glove. This process is referred to as "making in" by falconers. If this was a hunt for food for my table, I would entice her to leave her kill with a bit of food on my glove, and she would do it. My hawk trusts my actions will follow precisely according to all she and I have practiced together. She will accept my retrieval of her kill, done deftly and discreetly, and will never feel I have robbed her. Our partnership will remain intact.

How is it that this flying hunter does not resent my appropriation of her take? Raptor memory was explained to me in very simple, archaic terms when I was just beginning in falconry, but I wonder now if this explanation is broad enough to include other instances for which nothing but a remarkable memory can be responsible. Harris's hawks regularly provide jaw-dropping, incredible accomplishments on the wing. Sometimes it is a maneuver of agility like flitting through a rectangular opening six inches high and no more than four or five inches wide, at full speed, and not missing a wing beat. But these flyers surprise me also with memory much more grounded than I usually expect.

Every year I am invited to do a program for fifth-graders at a school near our home. I take Banshee, the New Hampshire School of Falconry peregrine, and a Harris's hawk to do the flight demonstrations. My Harris's hawks react favorably to repeating a performance in familiar surroundings. They have learned where they like to take perches in particular schoolyards they visit repeatedly, and they look for the same spots when they return. Their ability to remember those places was something I learned with surprise. Let one of their favorite landing spots be removed, and their reaction is almost comical. The bird heads for the phantom perch, now gone due to relandscaping, and circles tightly above the old location as if to say, "Hey, who took my perch??!" Since a flight demonstration at a school is an activity happening, at most, once a year, the interval between visits is at least a year in duration. Because I do not always bring the same hawks, two or more years can pass before they return to one of the schools. I do not expect them to have such excellent recall.

Knowing Harris's are capable of this type of perch recall makes me wonder why my falconry education taught me that a raptor's ability to create a concept is not within the realm of possibility. Let me explain. Imagine an ice-cream cone. Did you see it in your mind's eye? Was it chocolate, strawberry, or vanilla? Our brain can readily supply an image for familiar objects. Many falconers, including myself, have learned that raptors do not possess the capability to imagine something not there. This makes it possible to discreetly remove their kill without having them wonder where the lovely duck, chukar, or pheasant went. I know there is a great deal of truth in this. The effectiveness of making in when done right and the use of hoods are proof positive, but to me this is incongruous with a raptor's ability to recall a perching spot visited once and long ago.

I have been taught never to try to take something the raptor still has in his talons. The raptor's nervous system triggers an involuntary reflex of grasping when something they are holding moves. This ensures they will not lose what they have expended energy in catching. For the unfortunate falconer who has been grasped, there is no way out of the powerful clutch but to wait for the raptor's talons to relax and release. The harder one pulls, the tighter the raptor grips, so if it is your flesh with the talons in it, you learn not to pull back. If it is food or the lure you are pulling away, you are creating a negative image in the raptor's memory which is likely to ruin your chances of working with the bird because the bird *remembers* it. It makes me wonder if we just don't get the raptor brain at all.

We were at a falconry meet in Maine long ago when the subject of raptor intelligence came up and was being hotly discussed. "They're just flying lizards!" a skilled master falconer exclaimed. "They are not smart at all. They are *just flying lizards!*" I would accept his assessment with more finality if I had not heard him speaking later in the day. By then, this falconer was extolling how clever his falcon was!

The infallibility of the practice of "making in" has been proven to me many times, but never more so than on the day a videographer and a TV nature-show host were filming a segment on hunting with hawks. I was anxious to have my hawk and dog hunting together caught on film, as this is something many people do not realize can happen. We began as I released my pointer, Stormy, from her crate and she eagerly started quartering across the field, but having a microphone clipped to my vest, trying to coordinate a dog and hawk, hiking over uneven terrain, and answering questions from the interviewer all at the same moment was not a recipe for success.

We got three solid points on pheasant. Stormy was working methodically, but the videographer was having trouble keeping the camera on her while he was also filming the nature show host and me. With the cameraman between the dog and me, Jazz was distracted and was having trouble positioning herself for pursuing the pheasants we flushed. The three points, the flushes, and the chases came to nothing, but the videographer managed to get a good percentage of it all.

After five hours of filming, the day had grown hot. The dog was tired, and so was I. I knew the bird was tired, too. Jazz had worked just as hard, or harder, than the rest of us. She was now sitting high up in the top of a tree, enjoying what little breeze there was, and, I suspect, happy to be farther away from the strangers who had been following her all day. I finished watering Storm then kenneled her in the dog crate before I turned to speak to the host and the cameraman. "I hope you got enough for your segment. I am sorry we did not take game." They assured me they had plenty of film. All that was needed was footage of the host holding Jazz as she gave her wrap-up for the segment to air on TV.

"Well, that's fine," I answered, "but the bird has worked really hard today. Before you film her, I want to leave Jazz with a feeling of success." I explained I had a live quail in my pocket for the hawk to pursue. The long, unsuccessful day had been a disappointment for Jazz. I was not sure if the missed opportunities would be detrimental to our hunting relationship. I felt it was important to end her day on a high note. The videographer asked if he could film the sequence about to happen. "Of course," I told him.

Pulling the quail from the game pocket of my vest, I tossed it into the air. It took off as if jet-propelled and flew much higher than I had expected, right up to the level where Jazz was sitting in the tree. By the time it reached her altitude, Jazz was airborne as well. Her yarak was high, and she hit the quail hard. Feathers flew into the air, but it was a glancing blow as the quail turned in the air and headed for cover. Jazz whirled about in pursuit. I shouted to the cameraman to follow as I raced after the pair. Jazz had landed with the quail she had caught and killed. "She got it!" I called out kneeling beside my hawk while I attached each of her jesses to the clip of my hunting leash. The cameraman had been running along behind me, so he began filming.

I envisioned letting my bird enjoy what she had been working hard for all day. The TV host ran up to join us, saying, "Now take it away from her!" I could not blame her; I knew she had no way of understanding what I was up against in taking possession of a kill at that moment. I made no reply but instead began garnishing my glove with pieces of chick legs, chick heads, and chick bodies sticking out in a grisly smorgasbord. I lowered my glove in front of Jazz, just above the quail, and gave a whistle. Jazz dropped her quail and immediately came to the glove. Retrieving the quail, I handed it off to the host. The host and cameraman may not have understood how well my hawk had reacted in this situation, but I knew, and the knowledge thrilled me. This was a moment for me to savor my hawk as she ate the chick pieces on my glove.

CHAPTER 37

Crash

Normally when I am training a falcon, I do not welcome sightseers, but I was a guest using a field one day at the Timberdoodle Club when two members asked permission to watch. I bid them welcome, waving them to a small knoll nearby. "Have a seat over there if you would like to see her fly," I directed. The man and woman sat on grassy slope as I continued unhooding the peregrine on my fist.

The young bird was newly trained but had proven to be loyal to the lure and still was too new at the process of flying free to follow the definition of "peregrinate," which means "to wander." I held out my arm, she roused and then cast off into the air, gaining height by flying in tight circles. Around and around, using the knoll as her center point, she rose higher in the sky. I flew her until I was satisfied she had had enough and pulled out the lure to call her down.

Just before I swung the signal for her return, I glanced over at my spectators. The falcon had been flying in perfect circles above them as they sat, their heads turning in unison as they watched her. They had no idea that their faces, with their mouths open in amazement, mirrored one another. Watching a raptor fly is like learning to read; the more you watch, the better you are at catching every detail.

Two years following the summer I spent with Witch and N-Z, we were called to rehab a juvenile peregrine from the Tufts Wildlife Clinic. With this second wild peregrine, I had a chance to watch step-by-step the evolution of a juvenile trying its wings, learning what it could do with its instincts as it became an accomplished flyer and huntress. When she came here the young female was about fourteen weeks old, a very late age to be learning Flight 101. However, she mastered the basics and more at fast-forward speed.

This peregrine had become a casualty on her maiden flight. She had glided off the Brady Sullivan Tower in downtown Manchester to perch in a sapling across the street. Then she pivoted and launched herself into the air to return—directly into the windshield of an oncoming car. Fortunately the Brady Sullivan peregrines are closely watched by a group of dedicated volunteers. On this day, a volunteer was already on her feet running and managed to retrieve the stunned juvenile bird from the pavement. Chris Martin, Audubon's biologist, was duly summoned to take the bird to a rehabilitator for observation. In the meantime the fledgling watchers, Chris, and other Audubon staffers began calling the young falcon "Crash."

The rehab inspection turned up no wing damage, so Chris returned the bird to the tower. The next day the falcon-watching volunteers noted the juvenile was not attempting to fly. Something was wrong. Chris hurried to the rooftop, where the young bird had remained without taking part in the flights of her siblings. Chris told me later the injury had not affected her speed or her endurance, which resulted in a footrace around the roof before he finally managed to net the youngster. Once captured, she was taken directly to Tufts Wildlife Clinic, where an X-ray revealed a broken bone in her chest, a bone necessary for anchoring her flight muscles. The prognosis was excellent for healing without any lasting damage. The young bird's wing was bound, and she was kept at Tufts until the broken bone knitted. Afterwards, she was brought to us for training, conditioning, and evaluation.

Maturity-wise, the young bird was still at fledgling age, meaning she had little knowledge of her own flight capabilities. She was clueless in the hunting department, too. By now her siblings and parent birds were all over the city of Manchester, flying and hunting. Returning the young bird to the nest box tower would not initiate training on the part of her parents. Crash had missed the boat due to her injury. She came to us to rectify the problem, but she brought with her some bad manners. She bit whenever she felt like it, so my hands and forearms soon were covered in welts and small gashes. She had little fear of humans. In her favor, however, was that she was as typically independent and driven as others of her species. Soon after her arrival, she was negotiating flights from perch to perch within her mew. Free-lofting was very good for toning her flight muscles. After a while she had healed as though the interval of convalescence had never taken place. She was raring to go to the next phase. We started training immediately.

Working with the young wild falcon was not like working with Witch. For one thing, watching Crash as her level of maturity rose every day was a revelation in how quickly a raptor could move forward. With each flight and with each experience, she progressed as if the accident had not interfered with her development. Perhaps because she had been raised on a towering building, she had no problem being at a good height from the very first flight. There were no hair-raising adventures such as crossing Route 149 at a low level. She was adept at keeping altitude, even when the ground rose steeply below her.

One day Crash widened her circle to include a small field behind our house. I watched from the Overlook, where I had launched her. When a falcon wants to settle its feathers more neatly, it does something falconers call a "rouse." It fluffs itself up so that it resembles a large feather duster. Next, the bird gives a hearty shake, which smooths the fluffed feathers down into flight-readiness. Usually falcons do this while they're perched prior to takeoff. But I watched Crash rouse herself in full flight without missing a beat or losing altitude. Once she was shipshape, she resumed her sleek form and flew on. I was impressed!

In the hunting department, however, she had a lot to learn. On the first excursion to the Overlook, she spied a flock of sparrows feasting on something in the grassy field. As soon as Crash saw them, she got excited. She tried to bate off my glove before I had a chance to release her. She remembered sparrows! Obviously, Mom and Dad had brought them home for dinner at the tower. I unclipped the hunting leash and launched her from the glove, but instead of taking a hunting position by circling and gaining height, the greedy youngster flew directly to the middle of where the sparrows had been. "Had been" were the operative words. She looked about in puzzlement. There was not a sparrow to be seen. I could almost see the wheels turning inside Crash's head. *Hmmm. Bad approach. Don't do that again!*

Unlike my experience with Witch, the Overlook became a very satisfactory place to fly Crash. She utilized the broad valley below and kept her altitude as she flew over me on the hillside. She became swifter and more agile at catching the lure even when I tried to make it hard for her to catch.

Once we had her flying, Chris Martin came over one day to watch. Handing him my whistle, I invited him to enter the mew with me as I caught her up and slipped her jesses through the grommets of her anklets. I asked Chris to swing the whistle hanging from its lanyard near Crash to focus her attention on it instead of on biting me.

After rigging her with jesses, we walked up to the Overlook field. Chris had brought his photography equipment in a black nylon bag. He set it to one side in the field and readied his camera. I launched Crash.

At this point, she normally would begin a circle. But today was different. We had a guest who had brought along something that made her curious. She landed and walked over to lay claim to Chris's bag as a trophy. I began swinging the lure to call her off of it. Once she had footed the bag several times, tried to upend it, and finally reached the conclusion it was not going to yield anything she liked to eat, she accepted my invitation. "Do you think she is too used to people?" Chris asked with concern. "Will we be able to release her?" Chris was envisioning Crash attacking people carrying nylon bags.

"She is still a baby in her head," I answered him, "but she is changing rapidly. She can be a really ornery bird at times, and I think that bodes well for her going back to the wild without problems."

What I had predicted was exactly what happened. When the time came for actual hunting, she pursued game, caught it with gusto, and allowed me to make in and reattach my leash to her jesses as she fed. As Crash's skills improved, she progressed quickly towards maturity.

After two months with us, Crash was up to speed in both hunting and flying. One of her flights at the Overlook proved her ambition. She quit her wide circling of the field to concentrate on an area below where the land dipped steeply and met the forest growing at the foot of the hill. She went around and around over this area and then began to make half-stoops. She would circle and dive, only to pull out, and then repeat the process. I figured there had to be something of great interest she was watching.

She had been at this for a time when I decided to call her in. I blew the whistle and began swinging the lure. Crash reacted by zipping out of her small circle to widely circle the field, coming back to neatly catch the lure I had thrown into the air at her approach. She landed nearby and began to plume the quail body I had tied onto her lure. I knelt beside her. The absence of our silhouettes on the horizon was immediately noted by the mysterious "something" that had so attracted Crash. Within moments a pair of turkeys took wing from the spot to settle in the pines at the end of the Overlook. I could hear them gobbling back and forth and from their indignant-sounding turkey conversation, I imagined it translated thusly: *Thank heavens! I thought that falcon would never leave!*

Just then, four more turkeys broke cover to join the first pair. The gobbling by now was almost raucous. I had to laugh. Crash had managed to pin down six adult wild turkeys at the base of the hill. "Well," I told her in admiration, "you certainly are starting out for the biggest and the most. You are a typical teenager, after all!"

Very soon after, we released her at the Overlook field. I wanted to set her free close by, reasoning if she had difficulty she would soon turn up at my yard only a few feet away. We have never heard a thing about her since, so I harbor the hope that my ornery, greedy friend is having a wonderful life and raising lots of young peregrines.

CHAPTER 38

Well-Groomed

The white bird has been here for almost six months and has refused all my slavish efforts to supply her with opportunities to bathe. I have brought her bath pans and lugged heavy buckets of water, but she has ignored my preparations. I am in a quandary. Do white gyrfalcons abstain from baths?

With the first snowfall, I take her out to bask in the sun. These outings will soon be curtailed by nasty weather and by the fact there is no place in the yard to drive in the stake of her perch. The ground everywhere is frozen as hard as a brick. Finally I resort to where I suspect the ground is still soft. The colonial-style goosefoot garden by my doorstep is warmed every day from the sun, which shines on the bricks of the house. The stake for her perch goes easily into the garden soil resting beneath a mantle of eight inches of snow.

K.C. flutters from my glove to her block as I tie off her leash. I step away so she can enjoy her weathering-out excursion. She eyes the snow as I leave to complete my chores. I am engrossed in feeding my other falcons when Jim gives a shout, drawing my attention back to the big white gyr.

K.C. has jumped down into the snow and is happily rocking back and forth as though in a bath pan. She dives her head down into the fluffy drift and enthusiastically rears up to fling snowflakes onto her back. After a bit, she returns to her block and begins to groom. K.C. has finally taken a bath in New Hampshire.

One thing you learn when you are observing falcons, especially peregrines, is how much joy there is in the simple chore of bathing. I have never seen a bird enjoy it more than peregrines do, although most of our hawks and other falcons relish a bath now and then. Peregrines know how to make a bath into a festive celebration.

Picture sparrows gathered about a puddle. They will hop into the water, raise their feathers in a rouse, spread their wings, and duck their heads beneath the surface so the water runs down along their backs. Peregrines do exactly the same things. They will settle in a bath pan and go about this regimen until they are completely soaked, splashing water everywhere. When they are finally done, they flutter back to their perches, where they will give their feathers a shake and begin grooming. Once they have groomed for a while, they will eye the water in the pan and dip in three or four times before they are done. The bathing always ends with an extended period of carefully cleaning and separating each feather, rubbing their beaks across the base of their tail feathers where oil glands are in abundance, and then spreading the oil the length of each tail and primary wing feather. Peregrines utilize bath-time as a lovely exercise in keeping themselves immaculate and healthy, and it is always a pleasure to watch them at it.

Tabasco, the red-tailed hawk, was an inveterate sun-worshiper. He enjoyed the occasional bath, but he often chose wet, cold days to do it. Lots of raptors do. They seem perfectly comfortable taking baths in weather we would consider best for snuggling in a sweater. On hot, sunny days Tabasco wanted to be a solar battery. Flattened out on the grass, with his tail and wings spread out, Tabasco made full use of the sun's rays.

Of all our birds, the one I loved most to watch grooming was Mrs. Chicken, the lanner. She would twist herself so that she was facing backwards while she vigorously rubbed the oil glands at the base of her tail with her beak and then very methodically transferred the oil to each long feather by running it through her beak. Before she was done, she would accomplish a stretching program worthy of any yoga instructor. To finish, she would bend forward while half extending her wings up and above her body, holding them behind like the figurehead of a Rolls Royce. One at a time, Mrs. Chicken would lift a leg in a long, luxurious stretch lasting a few moments before switching to do her other leg. This was so graceful that I always thought of her as a prima ballerina.

Hawks are a mixed lot regarding baths and sunning. The girls, Smokey and Fire, enjoy baths, but they never get as into it as the peregrines do. Smoke and Fire wade in the bath pan, bowse (or drink) for a bit, do some rousing and rocking forward and back to dunk their tails, and then come out to groom. For some reason, the males, Scout and Sidekick, don't care for baths at all. Except for very rare instances, bowsing outside the rim of the bath pan is all they can be convinced to do. The Harris's go about grooming in a basic sort of way. Sometimes they will sun as Tabasco did. Other times they will sing, which sounds like rusty door hinges creaking.

On these days when my husband and I are "weathering out" our raptors, there is plenty to watch and hear as the birds engage in sunning, bathing, grooming, and songfests. It is a slow-paced, lazy kind of day, sometimes punctuated by a passing car slamming on the brakes in disbelief at the scene taking place on our lawn. We've had people pull into our driveway to ask questions about the school and then jump in surprise when the heads on what they had assumed to be lawn ornaments turn to watch them. The best thing about the activities I have just described is that they only happen if a raptor is comfortable in his surroundings. Knowing that our birds are calm and at ease is validation we are doing things right.

CHAPTER 39

Scout

Someone in a crowd of spectators invariably asks me, "Which is your favorite bird?" My answer is always that I do not have a favorite bird any more than I have a favorite child or a favorite grandchild. I wish sometimes for the same closeness with another Harris's hawk as I had with Injun, but I also recognize this closeness was because Injun was my only Harris's at the time.

If the person means favorite in terms of handling and hunting, my experiences with hawks and falcons have been very different. It is hard to find spaces large enough in New England to fly peregrines and gyrfalcons to fully realize their potential. Inland New Hampshire, with its woods and meadows, is perfect for flying hawks. If I had to choose a good spot to fly peregrines or gyrs, I would pick the wide-open spaces out west or the grouse moors of Scotland. But I do the best I can with the terrain available.

As much as I love working with peregrines, it is so much easier to grab a glove, slip the whistle lanyard over my head, claim my hawk from his mew, and head off into the fields or woods near my house, so I tend to fly hawks much more than I do the falcons. Working with more than one bird has its upside. It exposes me to so many different personalities and behaviors. Each one of the raptors I have handled has proven to be a unique individual.

If forced to choose with which of the birds I now have the closest relationship, it would be Scout. He is, in some ways, very like Injun. He has a similar independent streak, coupled with more caution than Injun exhibited. His hunting drive is strong, and he is a willing, able hawk. My experience in training him was so classic, rather like a textbook example of falconry technique, I often repeat the story when I am teaching a class about falconry.

I start by explaining that Scout trained very well from the beginning to the free-flying stage, which usually takes about three weeks. As soon as a free-flying hawk is returning on call and turning on its perch overhead to watch me, I begin to change my location. This prompts the bird to follow me, to keep me in view. A raptor has the instinct to watch whatever is moving about on the ground. At this point in training, the only thing moving on the ground ahead of him is me.

When I know the bird is following well, the next step is to get a "baggie." A baggie is usually a live quail in my pocket which, without warning, I will toss out ahead of me. The baggie will fly, giving the hawk a chance to pursue, and to catch if he is able. When the hawk sees me produce game, I become an entry into what I refer to as "the hunting-success file folder" in his brain. Flying after game I have scared up, or thrown out ahead, signifies the beginning of our partnership.

A hawk or falcon is not a pet but a hunting predator. In all we do with raptors, we are joining them in what is normal activity for them, not contriving something they are joining *us* in. It may appear that the falconer is strolling along with an attentive, flighted friend keeping her company, but this is not what is happening. The human is actually fulfilling part of the hunt for the raptor by being the disturbance on the ground instigating a chase. Should this activity of "following on" never result in game being flushed, the raptor would begin to seek prey farther afield, away from his human hunting partner.

On one day during his training, Scout was following on very well. I was happy with his progress, which prompted the thought, *Time to get a baggie.* But this was just a thought. After a few flights, Scout played a trick on me, one typical of a Harris's hawk. Instead of flying back to a tree branch overhead, he landed instead on the ground behind me. For him to be on the ground is bad for a couple of reasons. One, he is vulnerable to attack by other predators (or the neighbor's roving dog), and, two, he cannot see what is going on from down there. The solution is for the falconer to leave the spot, a maneuver requiring the hawk to change his location to keep the falconer in view. So I walked down towards our barn and made a ninety-degree turn. As soon as I was out of his sight, Scout sailed around the corner, passed me, and flew about thirty feet into the woods, where he landed in a small maple sapling. This was exactly the reaction I was looking for. I turned on my heel and reversed direction. Scout's bells tinkled, and then I heard him land in the large maple behind the big barn not far behind my shoulder.

Suddenly, I heard the bells again as they hit the ground. I turned to see a mouse tail flipping back and forth between Scout's talons! In my walking about, I had scared up a field mouse, and Scout had taken quick advantage of this. What a champ! No need to buy a baggie now. (But we did work to increase Scout's slips on game in order to cement that partnership between us.)

Scout, being a male, is more volatile than female Harris's hawks, and his sense of caution can send him to a high limb when something unexpected happens. One of these instances occurred during his initial training. My daughter, Marna, and granddaughter, Neave, had arrived to spend the weekend with us. Neave was six years old at the time. Their arrival came as I was finishing a session with Scout. Neave clambered out of the car and came running for me just as I called Scout down from a perch on a tree limb. My granddaughter and the young hawk were coming at me at exactly the same moment. I yelled to my grandchild, "Neave, go back to your mother!" Startled by both my tone and by nearly meeting Scout head-on, Neave turned and ran back towards Marna, and Scout wheeled about in the air and headed to the woods' edge.

It took a moment before Scout calmed down enough to come down to my glove. When I went in search of my grandchild, I found her sobbing into her mother's shoulder. I had never shouted at her before, and she was embarrassed, feeling she had erred in causing the bird to fly off. I felt badly about bringing my granddaughter to tears, so I hastened to explain she had done nothing wrong. It was just that Scout was a young bird full of his own fears. The sobbing turned into a wail.

"Oh, Neave, come along with me," I cajoled. "I have something to show you." Neave shook her head adamantly and reburied her face in Marna's shoulder. I worried Neave would never want to be around me when I was flying birds, and flying birds is what I do quite a lot. "Come on, honey, let's go do something fun." The wail subsided to a few shuddery breaths as I took her hand and led her down to the old stone wall near Scout's mew. I cast Scout off my glove to fly up to the mew roof, from where he watched us.

Taking a seat on the wall, I pulled Neave into my lap and slid my glove onto her hand. It went way up her small arm to nearly her shoulder. "Let me show you something, Neave," I repeated. I fixed a chick leg between the fingers of Neave's glove and blew the whistle. Scout responded instantly by flying down, but when he arrived and saw I had another creature on my lap wearing the glove, he did the fly-by maneuver and returned to his perch on the roof. Neave squirmed, taking this as failure on her part. "Hold still, Neave," I told her. "He was just surprised at you being here. He doesn't know yet if you are a safe place to land." Neave ceased wriggling and held her arm out.

I gave another whistle, and Scout sailed down. This time the presence of Neave was not a surprise, and he landed upon her glove and ate his chick leg. I heard a small, breathless voice from under my chin. "Let's do it again!" So we did.

Since then, while doing lots of classes, hunting, and event demonstrations, Scout's confidence has increased. He is becoming bolder, and I find he and I work together in a more finely tuned relationship. His reliance on our partnership became especially clear to me when we presented at a particular local event.

I had set up for a flight demonstration a short distance from where we had the birds on exhibit. Jim remained with the display while I walked Scout out to where I planned to fly. Before a flight happens, I go over every part of what I plan to do. I usually check that I have every piece of equipment I need and place a bag of tidbits in my pocket. This day was no exception, but it was a brutally hot summer day. Keeping our birds out of the bright sun as the available shade moved required constant revisions in perch locations. Prior to the flight demonstration, there were lots of interruptions, and my mental checklist did not keep pace with the detours in my train of thought.

As I walked to the flight location, I was playing a movie in my mind of how I wanted the demonstration to go. Once at the spot, I informed the crowd of where to stand, then I cast Scout off and reached into my pocket for a tidbit to find . . . nothing! This was potential for disaster if ever there could be. I had forgotten to pull the tidbits from the cooler to place them in my vest pocket. Scout flew to the woods' edge, where he took a perch on a shaded limb and turned to watch for my cue. Instructing my audience to hold their places, I turned quickly and hurried back to our exhibit area. I stepped over the tape marking our display and headed to our cooler.

Scout swooped down to land in the midst of his compatriots. He turned to me inquisitively. I am sure he must have been wondering why I had deserted him. Time stood still for an instant as we faced one another. I held out my empty glove and tapped on it with my right hand, which is one of our signals that draws attention to the glove, but that the glove does not necessarily hold food. Scout immediately flew up to my glove. It was clear he felt more secure being with me perched on his safe place, even with no tidbit.

With the packet of chick pieces in my pocket, I stepped out of our exhibit. My husband sent me a smile. "That was impressive," he said approvingly. Scout and I hurried back to proceed with the flight display. All the while I felt I was reliving a moment of my past. Something in my life had, unexpectedly, come full circle. The experience was so like having Injun back again after a ten-year space of time that it unsettled me, but it also warmed my heart.

CHAPTER 40

Peregrine Spring

We know when we've trained a raptor properly, it will react to us in a certain way, but, often lurking nearby, there is an element of disbelief, a distrust of our own abilities. Consider the apprentice falconer when the moment has come to loosen the creance knot, remove the swivel, and fly the bird free. Despite all he has been taught that a correctly trained bird at flying weight will return, the new apprentice has trouble believing it will happen.

Those of us who have passed the point when belief was abandoned know it suddenly becomes a terrifying leap of faith to remove the thin tether while testing the newly trained raptor on recall. It is the moment of truth, and the fear of failure gripping the new falconer the first time he releases a bird is something I think all apprentices must feel. Sometimes the apprentice's sponsor must step forward to speak reassuringly, and sometimes insistently, that the recall *will* be successful and it won't be the last time the apprentice ever sees his beloved raptor. This is something veteran falconers know, but each of us never forgets our own free-flight experiences when the mouth went dry, when the fingers fumbled in a moment of panic.

There was one Christmas some years ago when I faced disaster and my confidence flew away with the falcon. Jim was on crutches, the result of a fall that left him with a badly sprained knee. My son, daughter-in-law, and three-year-old grandson Kieron had already arrived for the holidays. I was in a rush to get the feeding of the birds over in order to concentrate on the family celebration. Jim was under orders to stay put with his knee up and iced. Out we went, me with Kieron in tow, laden with a bag of quail—full ones instead of halves because, as I told Kieron, falcons and hawks get Christmas presents, too.

The first mew we reached belonged to Jim's saker falcon, Sabretache. Sakers are exotic falcons native to the Asian deserts. Sabre, however, was hatched out of a propagation program in Utah. When he arrived, he was a handful. After Jim had manned him, however, Sabre became a sweet falcon to handle, although he was still high-strung and became startled quite easily. Jim's work schedule began to take him away quite a bit, so he asked if I would like to train Sabre. I enjoyed working with him, but once he was trained, I left off flying him, as I was very busy flying my own birds. As of that Christmas, Sabre had not been out to fly in a long while—many months, in fact.

Sabre is a raptor who always seems ready for food, and while this greed is an asset in training, it also makes him difficult to feed as we parcel out quail. His habit is to run around to get between the outside door and the canvas curtain that covers the opening, so when you open the door, there he sits. The first time this happened to me, my heart nearly stopped. I got the door shut quickly enough to prevent his flying out, but it was a close call. After that, I developed a way to bring him up to the mew window and away from the door. We save those crinkly grocery bags to recycle as hawk food carriers. I learned if I first unlocked his mew door, then stood at the barred window and chanted, "Hey, Buddy Boy!

Whoo-hoo!" while shaking a grocery bag, Sabre would fly to the window and leap up and down. At this point I would drop the bag as he tried to snatch it through the bars, run like mad for the door, and whip the food behind the canvas curtain into his mew.

On this Christmas Day, however, I had the assistance of a three-year-old. Once we had Sabre's attention at the window, I left Kieron holding the food bag, telling him to shake it up and down while I ran to fling the quail into the mew. Kieron shook the bag once and then became absorbed in his grandmother's histrionics. When I snatched the door open, I was face to face with a saker falcon whose gaze was riveted intently upon the quail I held in my bare hand. Reflexively, I slammed the door closed. The falcon turned, his wing dropping down between the door and the sill. Even faster than my slam-reflex was my grab-reflex, which caught the door before it closed on his slender wing. In the slow-motion in which disasters sometimes play out, my grab of the door edge tipped the quail from my fingers to land first on the door sill, then bounce to the step outside the mew. In a flash, Sabre grasped his Christmas-gift quail and flew off into the woods. "Gramma, the bird flew away," my wide-eyed grandson informed me.

I grabbed Kieron's hand as we raced to the house, where I gave him over to his mother with the admonishment of "Don't tell Grampa!" Outfitting myself with whistle and glove and stopping only to garnish a lure with quail, I headed outside to fetch my dog Stormy. I figured if I was lucky, Sabre would be feeding on his quail at the edge of our woods. I hoped Stormy could locate him before he had fed up, as it would be very difficult to retrieve an already plump raptor which had not flown much in nearly a year.

Within a few minutes my son, Chat, a non-falconer who had grown up with many of our birds, joined me to help hunt for the bird. Stormy's nose made a thorough investigation with no results. The wood-line was empty of any life. My son and I walked back to the house. "Mom, I can go farther in and keep looking," Chat volunteered.

"No, I think I will have better luck alone. Sabre is more at home with Dad and me than strangers. I want to try to sight him with no one else around." Chat returned inside while I kenneled Stormy.

I had little expectation of seeing Sabre again until the effects of a full repast had worn off, but as I rounded the garage, I gave a toot on the whistle and idly swung the lure. My scanning line of vision caught something above the field, up in the neighbor's yard on the far side of the stone wall, trees, and undergrowth dividing the properties. A falcon shape was rising, straight up into the air. I followed its progress heavenward. My jaw dropped. Was it possible Sabre was responding to my call? The next second I was facing a falcon stooping down at the lure and realized I was standing on pavement. Hurriedly I tucked the lure under my arm and ran for the field.

Sabre pulled out of his dive when the lure suddenly disappeared. Would he return? The odds were stacked so heavily against me, I thought the likelihood was very slim. I did not factor in all the time invested in carefully following the principles of falconry. Those techniques and the dedication to following them are what saved my day.

Once on softer ground, I swung the lure again. Sabre reappeared, barreling around the top of one of the tall spruces separating the field from the driveway. He was coming so fast, my heart jumped into my throat. At the apex of the lure swing, he hit it hard and grabbed. Instead of releasing the lure handle, I held on, and the lure came to land—quail, falcon, and all— only a few feet away. Without a moment's hesitation, I leapt for the jesses. In less time than it takes to say "God bless us, every one!" I had the falcon and his second Christmas quail deposited inside his mew with the door securely closed and locked. Then I went in and told my husband how I lost his falcon and got it back, all on Christmas morning.

Our raptors open up a world otherwise not visible to us. Jim likens this to carrying a flashlight into a darkened room. It is a given if one of our birds looks up, so do we. If I step out of the house on a day we have our birds perched out on the lawn and see one of them looking intently towards the sky, I know when I look at Jim, he also will be staring upward. Falconry has changed us, has marked us, in ways people who are not falconers have a hard time understanding. How does one explain to someone who has never flown raptors our feelings when a hawk or falcon has chosen *us* to trust or to follow?

N-Z was a peregrine any falconer would have loved handling. The remarkable steadfastness he showed when on his lure meant he trained easily and well, but in a wild falcon this behavior puts the bird at serious risk. Once N-Z had claimed his prize, he was not going to startle and fly off. This trait is beloved by falconers in the tame falcons they train, but likely was the cause of his being car-struck and killed. How wonderful if federal rehabilitation laws had a clause allowing a rehabilitator, upon recognizing such an inborn trait, to explain that this particular falcon would do better to stay in a falconer's care. Rather than being deemed "non-releasable" and left to sit in an exhibit for the rest of his life, this bird could hunt and fly as a falconry bird, and his chances of being killed on the road would be drastically reduced. In 2001, when I was working with N-Z, the suggestion that he go under a falconer's care, even temporarily, would have been met with immediate disapproval. Even today, now that the peregrine has been downlisted, there is no panel of wildlife judges to weigh opinion against regulation in such a case. I finally reached the conclusion that N-Z was doomed to another similar injury or to death very soon after being back in the wild. He was incapable of changing.

From Witch I learned so much. Like my young bird, I had been flying wantonly. It had seemed enough for Witch and me to throw ourselves into flight without a care in the world. I will never be so reckless again. It was a hard lesson. Now, many years later, my heart skips a beat when I pass that spot on the Souhegan River. My eyes still scan the sky above the mill complex of Wilton, looking for a falcon shape. I cannot stop myself from doing it.

Despite that year of sad endings, despite the entreaty of my friend not to "get more falcons," I went on to have more experiences with peregrines and other raptors. Not often after that did I have a peregrine spring, a season crowded to bursting with exciting happenings involving raptors. Every year, I would watch for the return of the peregrines nesting on the building in Manchester and on the cliffs of New Hampshire and wonder if circumstance would bring us the unexpected surprise of dealing with a rehab raptor, or if fate would bring us a new adventure with falcons. More often than not, the months of March, April, and May have passed by uneventfully.

But out of the blue, the phone rang one March evening—peregrine springs always start with a phone call—and I had to make a quick decision. I told the caller, "Don't call anyone else. Just give me two seconds and I will call you back." The man offering his falcon must have thought I had gone mad.

"Would I be crazy to take on an eight-year-old trained peregrine?" I asked Jim, while thinking, *I will be seventy-four by the time this bird gets old and dies!*

"No," he said simply. No wonder I love this man.

I went back to the phone and called the falconer with my response. "You weren't kidding!" the man laughed. "It really did take you two seconds!"

Weeks later, I realized the new peregrine was the age Witch would have been. The task before me was much harder than training Witch. Pearl, the beautiful gift-peregrine, was not an imprint, but a bird handled by another person from the time she was young and for eight years. This presented a huge challenge. Any of the methods I used that were unlike those of her former falconer unsettled this veteran falconry bird. She and I continue to become used to one another. I am learning her ways, and she is learning mine.

This peregrine has progressed to such an assuredness that she now greets us with vocalizations when we approach her mew. Although the eggs were not fertile, she produced two the spring after her first year with me. Last April she produced a clutch of five brown-speckled eggs. Her satisfaction with her new life is apparent.

My most profound experiences often come from the reactions of people we meet during educational programs. Their comments give me a sensory rush as I see the magnificence of our birds through new eyes. It takes my breath away. My husband is not so outgoing. He is more private, more introspective. His study of falconry throughout history is something he puts into context in his handling and training of our raptors. Extrovert married to scholar, we work and share with one another the best, and sometimes the worst, that can happen during the gamble of setting one's heart free to fly.

Over time I have come to realize the part of our lives given over to the birds and to flying them is an adventure. Would something else have supplanted this adventure had we not been falconers? Perhaps. But would I be the same person, would Jim, if it were not for the molding of our preferences, our personalities, and our lives by Injun, Witch, N-Z, Tater, Tabasco, Bubba, and the others? The answer, of course, is no. No matter the changes the birds have wrought in us, there is always more to learn, to do, and to experience. An old and very true saying in falconry has become our mantra: "It is not the man who trains the bird, but the bird which trains the man."

Life here with our raptors goes on with the sweet and the bittersweet. Each year is different. There are new goals and challenges, new fears and delights. A peregrine spring is no longer a time or a season, but a state of mind, a condition of living life immersed in the activities of working with our birds. I find our raptors have bestowed another truth upon me. As long as I have a hawk or a falcon to care for, to learn from, to fly, I do not have to wait for another peregrine spring to come. Peregrine spring has arrived.